"The most successful people on the planet have failed too many times to count; the only difference is they use that to their advantage. In this book, Jon shows us that failure is actually a key ingredient to success, provided that we are willing to learn from it. It's true that success can sometimes be a painful process, but the rewards are worth the pain!"

—Kris Pavone,
Business Mentor and Life Coach,
www.krispavone.com

"J.K. Rowling describes the rejections she received before finally publishing her first Harry Potter book. Persisting in the face of failure can feel overwhelming. Jon's personal story provides practical steps to learn from our failures and become successful."

—Dr. Robin Morgan
Professor of Psychology,
Indiana University Southeast

THE
FLUNKED-OUT
PROFESSOR

Six Steps to Turn
Your Big Failure
Into Bigger Success

JON R. BECKER

AUTHOR
ACADEMY elite

Published by Author Academy Elite
P.O. Box 43, Powell, OH 43035

www.AuthorAcademyElite.com

Paperback ISBN-13: 978-1-64085-435-2
Hardcover ISBN-13: 978-1-64085-436-9
Ebook: 978-1-64085-437-6

Library of Congress Control Number: 2018956970

For Katie

I am so blessed!

TABLE OF CONTENTS

PART THREE: SUCCESS

FOREWORD

When Jon Becker asked me to write a foreword for this book, I asked, "You mean, tell everyone what a screwup you were back in high school? Because MAN, were you a screwup."

You can't pass up that kind of straight line with someone you've been friends with for four decades.

What makes Jon's story useful, though, is not just the way he has overcome early disappointments to achieve success. It's how universal the first part of his story is.

Not all of us have flunked out of college. But all of us, at some time in our lives, have encountered failure. In fact, most of us, if we're being honest with ourselves, have failed at something big, and for reasons that had everything to do not with our stars, but with ourselves. We fail to take a task seriously. We fail to think through the long-term consequences of our actions. We become too convinced of our own magnificence, too intoxicated with overconfidence to take note of the flashing warning signs around us. We tell ourselves the rules don't apply to us. We double down on bad bets instead of cutting our losses. And the next thing we know, we're failures.

In particular, many of us have encountered failure in high school and college, because adolescence is a roiling cauldron of all those counterproductive behaviors. As Donald Rumsfeld would put it, we don't know what we don't know. It's the job of the adults in our lives to keep us from failing in truly cataclysmic, life-altering ways, but that still leaves teenagers free to discover for themselves some of the bad things that happen when you do what feels good in the moment because the future is unimaginably distant. We discover, in our immaturity, that we are not, in fact, the culmination of God's plan, but vulnerable to the same flaws as all our ancestors back to Eden.

There's a reason director Amy Heckerling titled her high-school reimagining of Jane Austen "Clueless." It was in those clueless high school years that Jon and I met. We bonded over our fondness for music, theater, and the Chicago Cubs, which at that time was still an unrequited love. It's true that our teachers, if asked to predict Jon's future, probably would not have picked Jon as the one who would go on to a teaching career of his own. But neither would they have predicted him as the author and central character of a book with "flunkout" on the cover. This isn't one of those stories where all the neighbors tell the media that they knew the guy was a time bomb – and that's precisely the point. Some of our failures are easily foreseeable, but others creep up on us a step at a time – a decision that doesn't work out, a spontaneous decision to blow off a responsibility, a bad break at an inopportune moment – until we find ourselves flat on our back, wondering how the ground came up so fast to meet us.

Often, we react in those moments by cursing other people or our own rotten luck. Sometimes, that's even partially true. But it doesn't do a thing to get us back on our feet.

Jon has been there because we've all been there. We haven't all succeeded in the same ways; in fact, since you're holding this book right now, perhaps you're still searching for reassurance that there's not just light at the end of the tunnel, but any exit from the tunnel at all.

"Don't give up" would make for a very short book, though it's a necessary starting point. What Jon has demonstrated is how to make the next chapter one of triumph over our failures and flunkouts: taking stock of your abilities and maximizing them, recommitting to doing what's necessary to hold the line until you can begin to make headway, and surrounding yourself with supportive people who keep giving you encouragement along the way. I'm happy Jon and I have been there for each other in our "flunkout" moments. I think you'll be happy to discover Jon is there for yours.

Eric Berman
Indianapolis, Indiana
2018

INTRODUCTION

LOST

I never wanted to be a cruise ship janitor, a private investigator, or a truck driver. And I definitely didn't want to enlist in the United States Air Force. But at age nineteen, those were some of the options I considered. I never imagined that I would one day become an award-winning college math teacher. My future looked depressing.

I went off to college just eighteen months earlier with high expectations for myself. I set goals I wanted to achieve, but unfortunately, I hadn't thought through many of those goals. They were impulsive decisions based on what those around me were doing. They were unrealistic goals that didn't tie into my passions and strengths. And, as a result, I found myself in a recruiter's office just one signature away from heading off to Air Force boot camp. What had brought me to this point?

I had been kicked out of college.

Colleges don't like to say that they're kicking you out. I got a letter saying I was academically dismissed for failing to make "satisfactory academic progress." The letter was the university's delicate way of telling me that I was a flunkout—a failure.

I felt very alone. All my friends had gone off to college and were accomplishing great things: scholarships, the dean's list, and all the perks that came with a successful college experience. Meanwhile, back at home, I had no direction, no motivation, and no clue what to do with my life. I hung out at a video arcade all day and delivered pizzas at night. I made enough money to keep gas in my car and take my girlfriend out for a movie on the weekends. Living like this was okay for a little while, but as the weeks turned into months, a sense of hopelessness began to take hold of my spirit. I saw no end in sight. For a year and a half, I wandered aimlessly through life—never planning more than a day ahead—trying to forget that I had no plan for what I wanted to do when I "grew up." I really *was* a failure.

Then one day, my girlfriend Katie sat me down for a talk. We had been together for three years, and we had started talking about marriage. But I was about to experience a cold, hard dose of reality.

"I don't care what you do with your life," she said. "But you have to do SOMETHING. I love you, but I don't want to marry a bum."

A bum. She called me a bum. I was devastated.

Failure is unavoidable. Everyone has experienced some level of failure in school—from missing the bus to bombing a test. The good news is that while failure is unavoidable, you *can* overcome it. Overcoming failure isn't always easy. The key is to learn how to navigate failures and use each experience as a steppingstone toward the lasting success that you envision for yourself.

As a high school senior, I had a modest level of popularity, a cute girlfriend, a car (ok, it was my dad's, but I could drive it whenever I wanted to), and a decent part-time job. Like most high school students, I thought that my parents were clueless and that I had life figured out. I went off to college with a vague notion about medical school rattling around in the back of my mind. I was going to be a rich doctor with a beautiful wife, a big house, and lots of terrific kids who would think that their father was the greatest dad in the world.

Eighteen months later, I was a college flunkout. I had a dead-end job, my friends were all away at college, and now, the girl I loved had told me to get my act together or she was going to kick me to the curb. I was depressed, and I saw no way out of the mess I had created for myself.

So, how does a college flunkout with no apparent future become one of the top teachers at his university—incidentally, the SAME university that had kicked him out when he was nineteen? It sounds like the plot for a bad novel or a B-list movie, and if it hadn't happened to me, I would find the whole story ridiculous.

I have been teaching and academically advising college students for more than 25 years. And as I listen to their stories of uncertainty, frustration, and fear, I am frequently reminded of my 19-year old self—a lost and uncertain young man, struggling to figure out where I was going and what I was doing, feeling like I had no one to turn to for help.

The feeling that no one was there to help me through my difficulties has disturbed me for more than two decades. Despairing college students who find themselves in need of help should never feel as if they have nowhere to turn. They are my motivation for writing this book.

In evaluating my journey from failure to success, I have identified six simple steps that carried me through the mess I was in. These steps can be applied in all of our lives—whether we are a struggling student, a disheartened employee, or a stay-at-home parent. And I know that if you continue to read this book with an open mind and apply each step to your own journey, you can discover the success you want for your life.

If there had been someone to walk with me through the uncertainty of my initial university experience, I may not have flunked out of college. Perhaps I would have experienced successes that I can't even imagine. However, it is my failures that have led me to the success I enjoy today. And in hindsight, I am grateful for each one of them. They have molded me into the person I am. I would not change those failure experiences for the world.

WATCH THE WHOLE MOVIE

Sometimes, we become fixated on where we are at a given moment in time, and we forget about the successes we have experienced in the past. The fixation on our current circumstances can make it harder to envision successes we will experience in the future.

For example, my daughter Kelly once went through a very rough time with a car she bought. It turned out that the car was a clunker and the person who sold it to her was a con artist. Kelly ended up losing a lot of money on that clunker, and she was miserable the whole time.

What's interesting is that she was right in the middle of planning her wedding to the man of her dreams, she was preparing to graduate from college with honors, and she had a job that she loved.

But that car was a snapshot—a *moment* of her life. And she was miserable in the middle of it.

Living in the snapshot is a common human weakness. I do this all the time. In fact, I'm doing it right now.

I'm a good math teacher. I connect with my students both academically and relationally. My evaluations are positive. Students are eager to sign up for my classes, which often fill up before anyone else's classes. But recently, I graded some algebra exams...and I found myself living in the snapshot of the moment. I was not happy with my students' progress. I started asking myself what I could have done better, and I began to question whether I really had what it takes to keep teaching.

> "YOUR IDENTITY IS NOT BASED ON YOUR WORST DAY. FROM GOD'S PERSPECTIVE, YOUR IDENTITY IS BASED ON A DAY THAT YOU HAVEN'T EVEN LIVED YET."

Instead of reminding myself of the successful students I have taught through the years, I was dwelling on the moment I was in, subtly allowing that moment to define my life.

In the words of my good friend, Tom Orsag:

> *"Your identity is not based on your worst day. From God's perspective, your identity is based on a day that you haven't even lived yet."*

So what can we take away from Tom's quote?

Your life is not a snapshot frozen in time. Your life is a film-strip, a motion picture in which YOU get to determine the outcome. Your best day is a day that you haven't even lived yet. So, let's start writing the story of *your* life—a story in which *you* get to be the star!

PART ONE: FAILURE

"Every successful person is someone who failed, yet never regarded himself as a failure."

— *John C. Maxwell*

CHAPTER ONE

"Failure doesn't come from falling down. Failure comes from not getting up."

— *Zig Ziglar*

JUST ANOTHER CELEBRITY MELTDOWN

He was at the top of his profession—the first choice for any project. He was young and had money, fame, and influence. He had received numerous accolades and awards for his work. Then one day, he found himself in prison—busted for drug abuse and violation of parole. His fellow inmates decide to capitalize on his fame by beating him up in prison. He was fired from his job, and no one else wanted to hire him. "He" is Robert Downey, Jr., currently one of the most popular actors in Hollywood.

In the early 1990's, Downey was a rising star. He starred alongside Mel Gibson in *Air America* and Sally Field in *Soapdish*. Eventually, he was cast in the biopic *Chaplin* as Charlie Chaplin, a role which earned him an Academy Award nomination for Best Actor. Downey was experiencing incredible success on the big screen. His personal life, however, was quickly going off the rails, taking his career with it.

Downey's descent into the abyss of drug addiction was seemingly preordained. Introduced to marijuana at the age of eight by his father, Downey had the deck stacked heavily against him from his early childhood. Drug use became a bonding experience between father and son. "When my dad and I would do drugs together," Downey said, "it was like [he was] trying to express his love for me in the only way he knew how."[1] Inevitably, Downey began drinking heavily and spending his spare time in pursuit of drugs.

In June of 1996, Downey was pulled over by police officers and arrested on felony charges for unlawful possession of a firearm, possession of heroin and crack cocaine, and driving while intoxicated. Three weeks later, under the influence of drugs, Downey mistook his neighbor's Malibu home for his own and casually entered, undressed, and took a nap in a child's bed. He was arrested for trespassing. A month later, he was sentenced to a drug rehab facility in Southern California, a facility from which he escaped a few days later. Downey was re-arrested and sentenced to a secure rehab facility, with a warning from Superior Court Judge Lawrence Mira that any attempt to escape would land him in prison. In November of 1996, Judge Mira sentenced Downey to three years of probation on his felony charges.

Less than three years later, Downey found himself back in front of Judge Mira for a third parole violation. By this time, he had attended six different treatment programs—all without lasting success. In pleading once more for leniency, Downey tried to explain his addiction to the judge. "It's like I've got a shotgun in my mouth, my finger [is] on the trigger, and I like the taste of gun metal,"[2] Downey said. The judge was not persuaded and sentenced Downey to three years in prison.

Initially, it seemed like his prison experience would change him. "There's no way to explain how spiritually debilitating it is to be taken out of the loop of your life. It's like dying,"[3] Downey told NBC News during an interview from prison. Downey served fewer than twelve months, and upon his release, successfully resumed his acting career—winning a Golden Globe Award for his work on the television show *Ally McBeal.* Unfortunately, he was still haunted by his drug addiction demons. Downey was arrested again for drug possession and fired from *Ally McBeal.* His marriage had been stretched to its limit, and Downey's longsuffering wife, Deborah, filed for divorce, taking their son with her.

Acting work dried up for Downey. Studios were unable to insure any projects that he was attached to because of his drug addiction and erratic behavior. After his last arrest in April 2001, Downey knew that he would likely be facing another jail sentence or court-ordered drug rehab.

Downey lost his family and his career. In a later interview with Oprah Winfrey, Downey discussed his failed attempts to overcome addiction, telling Oprah, "When someone says, 'I really wonder if maybe I should go to rehab?' [I would say to them], Well, you're a wreck, you just lost your job, and your wife left you. You might want to give it a shot."[4] After five years of substance abuse, arrests, rehab, and relapse, he was finally ready to work toward a full recovery from drugs and a return to his career.

In 2003, his old friend, Mel Gibson, took a risk and paid the insurance bond to cast Downey in his film *The Singing Detective.* Downey went on to star in several more films, including *Gothika, Kiss Kiss Bang Bang,* and *Good Night and Good Luck.* On the set of *Gothika,* he met one of the film's executive producers, Susan Levin. The two quietly struck up a romance, but Levin was unwilling to marry Downey unless he got sober and stayed that way. He agreed, and they were married in August of 2005. In 2007, Downey was cast as Tony Stark in the *Ironman* franchise. The first Ironman movie hit theaters in 2008 and grossed more than $580 million worldwide. Downey was on top once again and has since become the cornerstone of the Marvel Cinematic Universe—appearing in ten Marvel movies so far, with more on the horizon.

Downey credits his wife, along with support from his family, additional rehab and 12-step programs, meditation, and martial arts for his sobriety. In 2015, Downey received a full and unconditional pardon from Governor of California Jerry Brown for his prior drug convictions.

Although dramatic, Downey's experience is certainly not unique. The entertainment industry, the sports world, and history itself are filled with incredibly successful people— those with whom you usually associate success—that have experienced the kind of debilitating failure that would drive the average person to quit. Consider the following "success" stories:

J.K. ROWLING

The Harry Potter books comprise the highest-selling book series of all time, having sold more than 500 million copies. The eight Harry Potter films have grossed over $8.5 billion dollars in worldwide sales since the first film, *Harry Potter and the Philosopher's Stone,* was released in 2001. Harry Potter's creator, J.K. Rowling, is the world's richest author, becoming the first to ever be listed on the *Forbes* magazine "Billionaire's List"—a list she *fell off of* when she donated over 15% of her net worth to charities.[5]

MICHAEL JORDAN

Named to 14 NBA All-Star teams, Jordan won five Most Valuable Player (MVP) trophies, led the NBA in points scored ten times, won the Rookie of the Year Award, and was named the MVP of the NBA Finals six times. More than a decade after his *final* retirement (he retired *three* times!) "MJ" is still revered for his gravity-defying slam dunks and tenacious defense, and he is widely considered the greatest basketball player to ever live.

ABRAHAM LINCOLN

One of the most powerful speeches ever given was just 272 words long. And on November 19th, 1863, in those 272 words, Abraham Lincoln not only dedicated a battlefield and honored its fallen dead, but he cemented his legacy as one of the greatest presidents and leaders in American history. As he stood upon the battlefield outside the small town of Gettysburg, Pennsylvania, Lincoln offered comfort, consolation, and commitment to the embattled northern states and gave the Union Army the motivation to carry on, defeat the Confederate Army, and abolish slavery.

Did you know that Rowling, Jordan, and Lincoln all experienced colossal failure? Although each of them is best known for awe-inspiring success, they also experienced crushing failure— the type of failure that would cripple most people.

> "...BY EVERY USUAL STANDARD, I WAS THE BIGGEST FAILURE I KNEW."

J.K. Rowling fell into a deep depression after the tragic death of her mother and stopped writing her first Harry Potter novel. In the hopes of lifting her depression, she moved to Portugal, where she fell in love, got married, got pregnant, got divorced, and moved back to England—with a newborn baby to feed, no job, and no income. She finished the first three chapters of her first Harry Potter manuscript while sitting in a coffee shop. She sent it off to a dozen publishers—all of whom rejected her book proposal. Rowling said of herself in a 2008 commencement speech at Harvard University,

"…by every usual standard, I was the biggest failure I knew."[6]

Michael Jordan was famously cut from his high school varsity basketball team. Despite a stellar college career at the University of North Carolina, he was drafted third (not first) in the 1983 NBA draft. During his NBA career, he missed over *12,000* shots. He was trusted to take the game-winning last shot in a game and *missed* 26 times. He lost more than 300 career games. He even gave up superstardom in basketball for a couple of years to play minor league baseball—an experiment that famously failed.

Abraham Lincoln experienced massive business failure and lost numerous political elections on his path to the presidency. He didn't even attend the Republican convention in 1860, at which he won the nomination, because he thought he had no chance to win.

Fortunately, the stories don't end there. J.K., Michael, and Abe all overcame failure to achieve the success for which they are recognized today. Their achievements gave them fame, fortune, and influence, and cemented their place in society as examples of *successful* people—not failures.

Of course, these aren't the only examples of individuals who overcame crippling failure on their path to success. Consider the following:

- Stephen King threw his first novel, *Carrie*, into the trash after it had been rejected by more than 30 publishers.

- Walt Disney was fired by a newspaper editor because, "he lacked imagination and had no good ideas."

- Oprah Winfrey was fired early in her career from a job as a news reporter because a television producer said she was "unfit for TV."

- Elvis Presley was fired by Jimmy Denny, manager of the Grand Ole Opry, after his first performance. Denny told Elvis, "You ain't goin' nowhere, son. You ought to go back to drivin' a truck."

- Harrison Ford was told by movie executives after his first film that he didn't have "what it takes to be a star."

- Lucille Ball was considered nothing better than a B-list studio actress before being cast in *I Love Lucy*.

- Steve Jobs was fired from Apple, the company he co-founded.

- Theodore "Dr. Seuss" Geisel had his first manuscript rejected by publishers 28 times.

- Lady Gaga got dropped by her first record label after only three months.

These are just some examples that reflect a recurring theme defining the history of all successful individuals.

In order to achieve success, we must be prepared to experience *and overcome* failure—an inescapable part of the process. Those who accept this fact and persevere through their failures

> "SUCCESS CONSISTS OF GOING FROM FAILURE TO FAILURE WITHOUT LOSS OF ENTHUSIASM."

are more likely to succeed than those who allow their failures to knock them down. As Winston Churchill once said,

"Success consists of going from failure to failure without loss of enthusiasm."

We have all experienced failure—the kind that shadows our thoughts and causes us to doubt our own ability to succeed. For me, those failures started in high school...

MY BIG FAILURE

School was always easy for me up through 8th grade. I got mostly A's without really doing any homework, while trying to stay out of the mischievous trouble that came along with being a free-spirited, but overall pretty good, kid. Everything changed when I moved from the small town of Demotte to the "big city" of Crown Point, Indiana, right before my freshman year of high school.

I found that high school was different. By the time I realized that I really should be doing homework, I had fallen far behind. I gave up on trying to get A's and accepted B's with the occasional C. I became a master at doing just enough to keep my grades slightly above average.

About halfway through my senior year, my friends started talking about where they were going to college. Several had taken the SAT—I had never even *heard* of the SAT. I hadn't thought at all about what I wanted to do after high school; meanwhile, my friends were already being accepted into universities all over the country.

Fortunately, I was able to take the ACT—so I *could* go to college if I wanted to, but I still had no idea what I wanted to do with my life. So, I went to see my high school guidance counselor, Russ Keller.

Mr. Keller was a great guy who had always taken an interest in me, an underachieving student who didn't want to do my homework. He told me that there were tests I could take to help me discover my strengths and abilities, and he was willing to give me these exams, if I was willing to miss a day of classes to take them. Missing classes with the permission of my guidance counselor sounded great to me, so I eagerly signed up.

While I was waiting to start my tests, I began looking through some of the career literature in the guidance office. One of the pamphlets described a career in marine biology, and the colleges that offered marine biology were all in sunny, warm states like Florida, California, and Hawaii. I immediately decided that I was going to be a marine biologist.

Mr. Keller called me back to the testing room. This was in 1982, so I had to answer each question by scribbling in my answers on a Scantron form with a number 2 pencil...and with each question, I answered the way that I thought a marine biologist would answer. I worked through a whole series of tests. I even took the ASVAB (Armed Services Vocational Aptitude Battery). I was leaving no stone unturned in my new dream of becoming a marine biologist.

After scoring my tests, Mr. Keller shifted through several pages of information. He looked at me over the top of his glasses and then back at the papers, then back at me. Finally, he told me that the results were interesting. However, he said it in such a way that made me think I would find them anything BUT interesting.

"What's it say?" I asked, impatiently.

Mr. Keller smiled. "According to these tests, Jon, your best career path would be to become a high school science or math teacher."

I waited for the punch line. After a moment or two, I realized that there was no punch line. He was serious. Something in those tests had indicated that I should be a math or science teacher.

"Are you sure?" I said. I was shocked. Maybe the science option came up because I was trying to answer questions like a marine biologist. "Mr. Keller, I hate math. And have you seen my chemistry grades?"

"Jon, I'm just reporting the results. You can see for yourself right here." He proceeded to show me a bunch of data from my test results that really didn't mean anything to me. I got mad.

"Mr. Keller, when I walk out of this high school, I'm never going back into another high school again," I stated, probably more disrespectfully than I intended. "A teacher? No way!"

I left his office disappointed and feeling as directionless as ever. What Mr. Keller had told me made no sense. I was not about to listen to his explanations about the things on the test that pointed out why I would be a good teacher.

I spent the rest of my senior year bouncing from one extra-curricular activity to another, making sure my grades were good enough, but not doing anything to excel academically. I still had no plan, and the results of Mr. Keller's tests faded from my memory.

The night of my high school graduation, a family friend named Betty *gave* me $3,000 for college as a graduation present. She had overheard me mention once that I thought it would be cool to be a doctor (because they make a lot of money), and she wanted to help me reach my "goal"—a goal that I had never actually set for myself.

I was shocked and surprised…and I was *completely* ill-equipped to be a doctor. I didn't like science, I hated school, and I didn't have the passion or ambition to actually become a doctor. But I didn't consider those things at the time. All I knew was that someone was handing me college money and I wasn't going to say no. College was only $39 per credit hour back then, so this was a lot of money. I enrolled at Indiana University Northwest, jumped into my first biology class, and within a couple of weeks, fell into the same lazy patterns I had exhibited in high school: not doing my homework, not paying attention in class, and goofing around with my new friends.

My irresponsible behavior continued for a year and a half. It took just three semesters to squander my way through the money that had been given to me, and then I received a letter from IUN, indicating that I was not making satisfactory academic progress and inviting me to stop attending. I had been kicked out of college for bad grades.

I could always find a reason to justify my own responsibility for failure. I wasn't considering the long-term consequences of my actions; instead, I was simply living day to day—doing whatever felt good. Not surprisingly, when the letter of dismissal arrived in the mailbox, I still tried to rationalize away my own responsibility for failure.

It's easy to find ways to place blame elsewhere. When I struggled in college, it was always someone else's fault. Either the professor lectured too fast, or he put things on the test that he didn't talk about in class. I couldn't find a parking spot because the lot was full, or I got stopped by a train and I didn't want to interrupt class by coming in late, or, or, or…

It is never enjoyable to admit failure, which is why we so often seek to place blame elsewhere. It is even less enjoyable when the fault is entirely your own. But it is in these moments that we find the greatest opportunities for growth.

YOUR FAILURE

As you have read through these examples of failure, I'm sure your mind has been wandering back over the failures in your own life. We *all* have them, so there is no shame in admitting that we have been a failure on multiple occasions in our lives.

The difficult part is in facing up to our failures, recognizing where we are to blame, and finding a way to move through them into the successes that await on the other side. In his best-selling book *Failing Forward*, John C. Maxwell says, "Success on any major scale requires you to accept responsibility. In the final analysis, the one quality that all successful people have is the ability to take on responsibility."

Since you are reading this book, you are obviously someone who is committed to becoming successful. Congratulations! Everyone likes the *idea* of achieving great things, but most people aren't willing to do the hard work that it takes to succeed. They fall in love with the myth of becoming an "overnight success." Ray Kroc, multi-billionaire owner of McDonald's once said,

> "I WAS AN OVERNIGHT SUCCESS ALL RIGHT, BUT 30 YEARS IS A LONG, LONG NIGHT."

> *"I was an overnight success all right, but 30 years is a long, long night."*

Success doesn't happen overnight…or in a day…or a week or a month. Sustained success is found by making decisions that will occasionally lead through failure and then making regular, sometimes minute, course adjustments along the way. What most people fail to understand is that changes don't have to be that large to make a lasting impact on your success. In the same way, if you fail to make those minute course corrections, you may end up somewhere that you weren't trying to get to.

For example, if you fly from Chicago to Hong Kong—a distance of approximately 7,800 miles—the pilot will make dozens of minor course corrections along the way to ensure that you arrive at your destination. If the course of the plane is off by just one degree, you will miss Hong Kong by more than 400 miles!

SIX STEPS TO SUCCESS

If you have read this far, then I know one very important thing about you. You are the kind of person who is committed to overcoming your failures. So, are you ready to make the changes necessary to arrive at your intended destination?

From my own experience, I have identified six steps that led me through my failures and into the success I have achieved. These steps worked for me, and they apply to many of the people I have studied who have also experienced success after overcoming their own failures. I believe that they will work for you too, as long as you commit to give them an honest try and make a sincere effort to follow them.

These six steps are:

- STEP ONE: Face your Circumstances

- STEP TWO: Accept Responsibility
- STEP THREE: Cast a Vision
- STEP FOUR: Take the First Step
- STEP FIVE: Make Course Corrections
- STEP SIX: Celebrate Milestones

In the chapters ahead, we will dig deeply into each of these steps. My hope is that by the end of this book, you will accomplish three things:

1. Recognize the Cause of Your Failures

2. Resolve to Make Necessary Changes

3. Reimagine a Vision for Your Future

This may feel like a daunting journey when we are sitting at the base of the mountain. But when we get to the top, the view will be spectacular!

CHAPTER TWO

"The journey of a thousand miles begins with a single step."
"Setting goals is the first step in turning the invisible into the visible."
"The first step is [that] you have to say that you can."

STARTING ON YOUR JOURNEY

Everyone seems to have a phrase or a slogan intended to motivate others to just START: *start* a new diet, *start* saving money, *start* looking for a job. Author Jon Acuff even wrote a book about starting. It was called *Start*, fittingly enough, and it was a New York Times bestseller. The idea of starting is a noble one and is so compelling that more than 120 million people make a decision every year to start something new...on January 1. We call those decisions "New Year's resolutions."

New Year's resolutions are not a bad thing. Every year, people around the world resolve to:

- Quit smoking
- Start exercising
- Find a new job

- Eat healthy
- Read more
- Save money

and countless other things that will presumably improve their lives. Unfortunately, only about 8% of people who make a New Year's resolution actually succeed in their goal. It's not the *start* that is so daunting. It's being able to see that resolution through to the end—it's the ability to *finish* that separates those who succeed from those who fail. Ironically, Jon Acuff recognized this same tendency, so he wrote *another* New York Times Bestseller called *Finish*.

Unfortunately, I have often found myself among the 92% of people who fail to realize those goals. But I have found that by applying the steps in this book, I am far more likely achieve success than if I blindly forge ahead without a plan to reach my targets.

STEP ONE: FACE YOUR CIRCUMSTANCES

It's impossible to start anything new unless you recognize that your current circumstances are not going to achieve the results that you want for your life. Albert Einstein is widely attributed as the author of the famous quote,

> *"Insanity is doing the same thing over and over and expecting a different result."*

But when we are stuck in our circumstances, even when we are not satisfied with the current reality, it is sometimes hard to try something new in order to break free of the self-defeating cycle we find ourselves in. Often, it takes a catalytic event to make us face the truth, try something different, and move ahead.

These catalytic events can take a variety of forms. In examining the experiences of many people, including myself, I have found that they generally fall into one of three categories:

RECEIVING AN ULTIMATUM

An ultimatum is one of the most painful incentives for change. When someone else tells you that you better change or there will be consequences, it is embarrassing, even humiliating, and generally will force us to make a change, whether we think we are ready to or not.

"I don't care what you do with your life, but you have to do SOMETHING. I love you, but I don't want to marry a bum."

My girlfriend gave me an ultimatum. She told me to develop and execute a plan for *my* life or she was going to move on with *her* life—and I wasn't going to be a part of it. Katie's need for a secure future motivated her to offer me a life-altering ultimatum. At that point, I had to weigh whether our relationship was important enough for me to move from the comfort zone of directionless inactivity into an unknown future. It was a scary time for me—I was only 19 years old. I didn't know what I wanted to do with my life, but I knew one thing for certain—I wanted her to be a part of it. In retrospect, that ultimatum was one of the best things that has ever happened to me.

EXPERIENCING LOSS

Experiencing loss is an effective catalyst for change. Job, relationship, and financial losses are all motivators for making life-changing decisions.

In a well-known corporate example, Bernie Marcus and Arthur Blank were officers for Handy Dan, a home-improvement chain in Southern California. In 1978, Handy Dan was purchased by a corporate raider who fired both men.

Unfazed by this unexpected setback, Marcus and Blank decided to start their own home-improvement store based on an experiment that they had tried in one of the Handy Dan stores shortly before they were fired: a home improvement store offering discount prices on *everything*. They called their new store Home Depot. In less than ten years, they opened more than 100 stores and made over $2.7 billion in sales. Forty years after its founding, Home Depot is the top-selling home improvement store in America. Handy Dan went out of business in 1989.[1]

As a die-hard Chicago Cubs fan, I am intimately familiar with the pain of losing. The Cubs went more than 100 years without winning a World Series. Then, in 2009, billionaire and lifelong Cubs fan Tom Ricketts, and his family, bought the team. They were determined to make whatever changes were necessary in order for the Cubs to become World Champions. In 2011, Ricketts hired Theo Epstein, the baseball executive who had turned the Boston Red Sox into champions after an 86-year drought.

Epstein determined the only way for the Cubs to reverse their "tradition of losing" was to strip the team of all its high-priced, underperforming players and rebuild the minor league farm system from scratch with young players—a process he stated would take at least five years. Long-suffering Cubs fans were used to losing, but the prospect of five more years of "losing on purpose" was discouraging, to say the least. Many fans abandoned the team, and, while I remained a fan, it was admittedly hard to watch the team I loved be so awful.

Epstein tore down the team, as he said he would—trading away overpaid players for minor leaguers who wouldn't make it to the major leagues for years. In 2012, the Cubs lost 101 games, their worst season in more than 40 years.

But in 2015, the Cubs won 97 games, making it to the play-offs a year ahead of their self-proclaimed five-year schedule. They eventually went all the way to the National League Championship Series before falling to the New York Mets. And in 2016, the Chicago Cubs finally broke their 108-year run without a championship by defeating the Cleveland Indians in what is widely considered to be one of the greatest World Series Game 7's of all time. The Cubs were finally world champions. But it took several more years of losing before they were able to make all of the changes necessary to finally attain their goal of a World Series Championship.

HITTING ROCK BOTTOM

Hitting rock bottom is frequently the culmination of the two previous categories. While one can be given an ultimatum or experience loss *without* hitting rock bottom, it is rare that someone will hit rock bottom without experiencing one or both of these situations.

"Rock Bottom" simply describes the place in life where things cannot possibly get any worse and the only way to go is up. It is often used to describe the point where an alcoholic or drug abuser finally reaches out for help. In an article in Inc. magazine, Thomas Koulopoulos, founder of the Delphi Group, writes that, "Hitting rock bottom…is when we learn life's greatest and most important lessons on which to build our success…I've become convinced that these lessons represent life's greatest opportunities to grow, learn, and innovate ourselves."

> "REMEMBER THAT JUST BECAUSE YOU HIT BOTTOM DOESN'T MEAN YOU HAVE TO STAY THERE."

Robert Downey Jr.'s story is an example of someone whose life had finally reached its lowest point. Filled with despair but coupled with the hope of a new life with Susan Levin, he was finally able to get the help he needed and climb out of his personal pit. Of his experiences, Downey later said,

"Remember that just because you hit bottom doesn't mean you have to stay there."[2]

While tales of recovering alcoholics and drug users are inspiring and often appear as feel good stories on the nightly news, hitting rock bottom also reflects the emotional, mental, financial, or spiritual state of someone who has received an ultimatum or experienced loss—the loss of a relationship, a job, or our health.

Here are a few examples of successful people who overcame their own "rock bottom experience."

LEWIS HOWES

Lewis Howes is a former All-American football player and decathlete. At one time, Howes held the record for most receiving yards in a collegiate football game in NCAA history—having caught 17 passes for 418 yards in a game.

Lewis left college a year early to try professional football. Two games into his first Arena League season, he collided with a wall and snapped his wrist, ending his football career. Major surgery soon followed.

There wasn't a huge market for former professional football players with no college degree and a broken arm. Penniless and without prospects for his immediate future, Lewis had hit rock bottom. He lived on his sister's couch for the next year as he struggled to find direction in his life.

Fortunately, the discipline and motivation that had made him an All-American athlete gave him the drive to define his future. Armed with his laptop, Lewis searched the internet day after day, studying entrepreneurship and leadership—learning from others how they achieved their own success. And as he applied the information he learned, he began to grow a network of businessmen and women. Eventually, he built a prosperous coaching business. Today, Lewis Howes is a best-selling author, and his podcast, "The School of Greatness," is in the iTunes top 100. And it all began when he broke his wrist playing football.

LOUIE ZAMPERINI

In her best-selling book *Unbroken*, Lauren Hillenbrand tells the inspiring true story of Louie Zamperini, an Olympic sprinter and U.S. Army Air Force officer who was captured during World War II and held in a Japanese prison camp for more than two years. When the war ended, Zamperini returned to America and tried to resume his life. But the Post-Traumatic Stress Disorder he suffered from due to torture endured while in captivity drove him to alcoholism. He vowed revenge on the Japanese prison guard who brutalized him mercilessly. Zamporini went so far as to plan a trip to Japan, where he intended to hunt down and kill his former tormentor. Eventually, Zamporini's PTSD drove him to become emotionally and physically abusive to his wife.

Then one night in September of 1949, a young, unknown minister named Billy Graham came to Los Angeles to share the gospel of Jesus Christ. Zamporini grudgingly went with his wife to the tent revival and listened to Graham talk about the love and peace that can be found in a relationship with Jesus. That night, Louie Zamperini hit rock bottom…and started an ascent that radically changed *his* life and the lives of countless thousands around the world. He accepted Jesus Christ as his personal Savior, and spent the rest of his life sharing his redemption story with others.

In 2014, Angelina Jolie turned Zamperini's heroic story into a major motion picture that was nominated for a variety of awards, including three Oscars.

DWAYNE "THE ROCK" JOHNSON

Most people think that Dwayne "The Rock" Johnson, one of Hollywood's most popular action stars, rose to fame as a result of his success in professional wrestling. While that is partially true, "The Rock's" success is actually rooted in his own failure.

Many of Dwayne's teammates on the football team at the University of Miami went on to fame and fortune in the NFL. Unfortunately, an injury during his senior year kept him from being drafted. He went onto the Canadian Football League on a practice squad contract that paid him only $250 per week, and he was cut soon after.

His dad picked him up at the airport after a long flight from Calgary, Alberta. As they drove back to his parents' apartment, Dwayne reached into his pocket and counted the money in his wallet. He had $7.00 to his name. It was at that moment when Dwayne "The Rock" Johnson hit rock bottom. He later dubbed this his "Seven Bucks Moment."

Vowing to turn his fortunes around, Dwayne decided to follow in his father's footsteps and become a professional wrestler. He began to train voraciously, and he eventually caught the eye of Vince McMahon, owner of World Wrestling Entertainment. Dwayne's spectacular rise to the top of the WWE and his massive success as a top Hollywood actor came from a moment when he decided that $7.00 was not going to define his future.

A CRITICAL STEP

Facing your circumstances is a necessary first step in overcoming failure. It is also the most difficult. No one wants to admit that they are living a failed life.

When I was hanging out at the video arcade and delivering pizzas, I was vaguely aware that my life wasn't really going anywhere. But I was comfortable. Someone else (my parents) provided me with a place to sleep and food to eat, and there was an extra car for me to drive. All I had to do was cover the gas and make a little money on the side. Mom and Dad didn't hassle me about my life choices—they pretty much let me make my own decisions. I had all the freedom of being an adult with none of the responsibility. Essentially, I was living my life as an extension of my high school experience without having to go to school. Why *wouldn't* I be comfortable?

The reality was far different. I was losing the respect of the person who loved me most, and internally, I was spiraling into a dark depression. My sense of self-worth was completely gone. I had lost all confidence in my ability to succeed at anything, and I had no idea how to reverse the course of my life.

In hindsight, I know the ultimatum that started turning everything around was a *gift*, not a curse. The pain of that statement was the external force that caused me to step back and assess my future. I had to face the reality of where I was in life, how it was affecting those I loved, and what I needed to do to put my life on track.

J.K. Rowling famously stated,

> *"Rock Bottom became the solid foundation on which I rebuilt my life."*

I couldn't agree with her more. When we find ourselves sliding down to places we never wanted to go, it usually feels like there is no end in sight—there is no bottom.

Fortunately, that is not the case for the vast majority of people. As any physics professor will tell you, everything is either in motion or at rest. If something is moving forward and then changes direction, there is a very *brief* point where it has to be at rest before changing directions.

Anyone who has come through failure to reach success will tell you that there was a point where they finally faced their circumstances and said, "That's it. I can't do this anymore. I do not want to live like this any longer. I have *got* to make a change."

"ROCK BOTTOM BECAME THE SOLID FOUNDATION ON WHICH I REBUILT MY LIFE."

For Dwayne "The Rock" Johnson, it was his "Seven Bucks" moment. For Louie Zamperini, it was in a tent in Los Angeles where he found Jesus Christ. For Lewis Howes, it was when he found himself living on his sister's couch with no prospects for the future. And for me, it was when my girlfriend told me that she was not going to marry a bum.

Franklin D. Roosevelt once said, "When you reach the end of your rope, tie a knot in it and hang on."

If you have hit rock bottom, if you have finally reached the place where you can't go any further on the same negative path, then I want you to tie a knot in your rope and hang on. Because soon it will be time to start climbing.

CHAPTER THREE

"Parents can only give good advice or put them on the right paths, but the final forming of a person's character lies in their own hands."

— *Anne Frank*

FIGURING OUT WHO'S TO BLAME

The easiest place to look when things are going bad is somewhere else. When we get a ticket for speeding, it's easy to blame the police officer for pulling us over. When we fail a test, it's easy to blame the teacher for how they grade. When we get called out on strikes, it's easy to blame the umpire. Whenever there is another place where we can shift responsibility, it is easy to find comfort in playing the blame game.

STEP TWO: ACCEPT RESPONSIBILITY

The natural result of facing our circumstances is recognizing that *we* hold the keys for change in our own hands. We can no longer cast our problems someplace else. We have to look ourselves squarely in the eyes and say, "No longer will I blame others for my own situation. It's my life, it's my problem, and it's up to me to fix it!"

This was the sobering reality I faced when I got kicked out of college and later realized that I was about to lose my girl-friend. It wasn't *her* fault that I had lost any sense of direction. It wasn't my *professors'* faults that I had gotten kicked out of college. In fact, it wasn't even the university administration's fault when they made the decision to kick me out. I had been placed on academic probation and warned in writing that my grades needed to improve for me to stay in college—twice! I ignored the warnings, and as a result, I suffered the consequences of my inaction.

Oddly enough, there is a liberating feeling when we finally become willing to accept responsibility for our own condition. When we continue to blame others for our troubles, we subconsciously expect that others will also free us from those same troubles. But when we accept the fact that *we* are completely responsible, we can then fully embrace the reality that only *we* can rescue ourselves from our current condition.

THE THIEF

I have known Bill* for many years. A very close friend through-out high school and college, Bill shared some of the same struggles with sense of direction and purpose that followed me when I had been kicked out of college. This led Bill to make some rather poor decisions.

Bill, like me, had gone to college, but it hadn't worked out the way he had hoped. So he got a job at a small pizza restaurant and eventually worked himself up to night manager. The

---

* Names have been changed

restaurant did most of its business through carryout orders, so the only person that worked at night with Bill was the delivery guy: Sam. Bill was responsible for waiting on tables, cooking the food, clearing tables, washing dishes, and closing up.

The store owner, Steve, paid everyone in cash at less than minimum wage. Bill thought this was unfair, so he devised a plan to start skimming cash from the nightly sales. When customers came into the store to eat, Bill would write up two receipts—one that would charge the customer the full amount, and a second one that he would put into the cash register for Steve to see the next day. Bill would pocket the difference between the two receipts for himself; he was a thief.

Bill had been raised with a strong moral compass, and he knew the difference between right and wrong. He acknowledged the nagging voice in his head that told him he was stealing. But he rationalized that the store owner was stealing from his employees by not paying minimum wage. He further rationalized that the reason they were paid in cash was so that Steve could get by without declaring all of his sales on his income tax return. Bill had no basis for this conclusion, but it made him feel better about stealing money, rationalizing away his own guilt by convincing himself that he was stealing from a thief, so it was okay.

This strategy lasted for a few months. Knowing deep in his heart that what he was doing was wrong, Bill kept track of how much money he stole. He told himself that one day when he could afford to, he would pay Steve back. Bill eventually stole about $300. And then, he was discovered.

Steve had started to notice that certain key food supplies were disappearing at a higher rate on Bill's shift. The receipts and the amount of food being used didn't add up. So, Steve started doing a food inventory before and after Bill's shift. Sure enough, Steve discovered a huge discrepancy. He confronted Bill about the missing food and the money that should have been in the cash register to account for it.

Bill was stunned that he had been found out. He immediately went into denial mode—stating that he had no idea what had happened. Steve pressed Bill to admit he was stealing, but Bill refused to accept responsibility. In one of the lowest moments in Bill's life, he pointed the blame for the missing money at Sam, the delivery guy—a quiet man with an excellent work ethic who would *never* steal from anyone.

Steve fired Bill on the spot. As he stormed out of the restaurant, Bill shouted over his shoulder, "Give me a call when you find the real thief!"

Bill carried anger, guilt, and shame with him for years. He wrestled with the character defects that caused him to become a thief, and a liar. And as these feelings gnawed at him, he knew that he needed to make right the wrongs he had committed.

Eventually, Bill went back to college, got a good job, and became a respected employee. He got married and had a couple of kids. But the guilt over his youthful failings kept eating away at him.

Finally, Bill knew that he couldn't ignore his past wrongs any longer. Twenty-five years after being fired for stealing, he told his wife, Sue, the whole story. He confessed to stealing, lying, and falsely accusing his co-worker. He told Sue that he had to try to make restitution. He needed to confess to Steve about what he had done and make financial amends for his theft. Bill needed to accept full responsibility and any consequences that might arise from his past actions.

Although they did not have a lot of extra money on hand, Sue fully supported Bill's decision to track Steve down and pay him back. Bill scraped together $400—more than the amount he had stolen—and started searching for his former boss.

It was a short search—Steve had closed the restaurant two decades earlier, but he was still living in the same house in a nearby town. Bill nervously dialed Steve's number.

"Hello?" Bill recognized Steve's voice immediately.

The words came tumbling out in a rush. "Hi, Steve. I don't know if you will remember me or not. My name is Bill. I was one of the night managers at your restaurant twenty-five years ago. You fired me for stealing." Bill's hands were shaking and his voice quavered as he spoke to the man from whom he had stolen so long ago.

"Yes, I remember you," replied Steve. There was no anger or judgment in his voice—simply an acknowledgement of fact.

Bill plowed ahead. "You accused me of stealing money, and I denied it. In fact, I tried to blame the delivery guy."

"Yes, I remember." Steve's voice was calm.

"Well, I have carried guilt around for the last twenty-five years. I *did* steal from you. I knew it was wrong, and I have felt so ashamed for so many years. I wanted to call you and confess to you that what I did was wrong. I am so sorry."

Bill took a breath, and before Steve could reply, Bill anxiously pushed ahead, "I always planned to pay you back. I actually kept track of how much I took. It was around $300.00. I want to send you a money order to pay you back, plus a little bit extra. You see, I am a Christian, and I know that what I did was a sin. God has forgiven me, but I still need to make restitution for my wrongs. Can I have your address?"

There was a pause on the other end of the line. Finally, Steve spoke.

"Thanks for calling, Bill," Steve said, kindly. "If God has forgiven you, then so have I. You don't need to pay me back."

Bill choked up. Fighting back the lump in his throat, he replied "Thank you so much for your forgiveness, Steve. I am *so* grateful. But I *do* need to pay you back. I need to make amends for my actions. I have a money order already made out with your name on it. I just need to know where to send it. If you don't want the money, you can donate it to a charity. But for my own peace of mind, please, let me pay you back this money."

Steve relented and gave Bill his home mailing address. Bill thanked Steve once more for his gracious kindness and hung up. Printing Steve's address carefully on the envelope, Bill added a stamp, dropped the envelope in the mailbox, and finally brought to a close the unfortunate incident that had haunted him for 25 years.

Or so he thought.

A few months later, Bill was leaving work. To get to his car, he had to walk through the conference center in the building adjacent to his office complex. He noticed that it was currently being used for a community arts and crafts show. Wandering through the exhibits, Bill came to one table that contained the most beautiful, intricately carved pieces of woodwork that he had ever seen. Most of them were woodland creatures, and Bill's eyes fell on a stunning carved owl. Bill was in awe—he looked up at the vendor who was sitting behind the table... and looked straight into Steve's eyes.

Bill felt his own pulse quicken. He could tell that Steve didn't recognize him. But Bill would have known Steve anywhere. He had been carrying guilt around for so many years, and he had only very recently been able to let it go. He would never forget that face.

Steve smiled and said, "Do you see anything you like?"

Bill thought about just commenting on the beautiful carved owl and walking away. But he *knew* that this was a Divine appointment, a God-moment—the chance to look his former boss directly in the eye and bring complete and total closure to the sins of his past. If he didn't seize this opportunity, he would regret it for the rest of his life.

Stammering, he said, "Steve, it's me, Bill."

Steve looked at Bill and recognition flooded his eyes. "Bill!" Steve said with a smile. "How are you?"

Bill smiled. There was no condemnation in Steve's voice. He sounded genuinely glad to see Bill.

"I'm doing really well, Steve," said Bill with a smile. "I'm doing a *lot* better than I would be doing if I hadn't called you a few months ago, and then I bumped into you unexpectedly like this!"

Steve chuckled at the thought. The two men chatted for a few minutes. Before Bill left, he reached out to shake Steve's hand.

"Thank you again for your kindness, Steve," said Bill. "I appreciate you not holding a grudge over the stupid behavior of an immature teenager."

Steve grasped Bill's hand firmly. "Not at all, Bill. We all make mistakes."

Bill and Steve went their separate ways, never to connect again. But on that afternoon, Bill finally felt the *complete* sense of healing that comes when someone you have wronged offers you genuine forgiveness. And it all began when Bill accepted responsibility for his actions.

AN INTERNAL DECISION

Accepting responsibility for our past mistakes is a deeply personal step that must occur internally first. It is not fun. It is usually painful. But it is necessary if we are going to move beyond our pain so that we can live life to its fullest.

The pain of our past mistakes is like an anchor that weighs us down and prevents us from experiencing the freedom that will allow us to soar. While we may not realize it in the midst of our shame, we cannot move forward until we fully release ourselves from our guilt.

"YOU CANNOT ESCAPE THE RESPONSIBILITY OF TOMORROW BY EVADING IT TODAY."

Once we have experienced failure and recognized our circumstances, it's essential we immediately and decisively take full responsibility for turning our life around. Abraham Lincoln once said,

> "You cannot escape the responsibility of tomorrow by evading it today."

Procrastination will not move us out of our circumstances. Only swift action to take responsibility for where we are will move us in the right direction.

For me, that swift action was to return to college so that I could eventually have a career that would support a wife and family. For Bill, it was making amends for past wrongs that kept him from being able to accept himself as a man worthy of forgiveness—both from the one he stole from and from himself.

We have all experienced at least one devastating failure in our lives that has altered the trajectory of our future. You may still be living in the aftermath of that failure—stuck in a place that you don't know how to escape.

You may need to seek the help of a trusted friend or a professional counselor to help you fully understand where and how you need to take personal responsibility. Step 5 of the Alcoholics Anonymous 12-step program instructs the individual to "Admit to God, to ourselves, and to another human being the exact nature of our wrongs." Admitting failure to another person is not always easy, but it might just be the key to moving ahead on your road to success.

Wherever you are on the road from failure to success, you need to examine your heart, recognize where you have made mistakes, and accept responsibility. It's one of the most critical steps on your success journey.

PART TWO: RECOVERY

"There are no mistakes. The events we bring upon ourselves, no matter how unpleasant, are necessary in order to learn what we need to learn; whatever steps we take, they're necessary to reach the places we've chosen to go."

— Richard Bach

CHAPTER FOUR

"Let's see what's out there."

—*Captain Jean-Luc Picard*

IMAGINE THE POSSIBILITIES

I love the above quote from *Star Trek: The Next Generation*. Captain Picard is about to embark on his first journey with his new crew of the U.S.S. Enterprise-D. He could only imagine what mysteries lie beyond the stars.

Much like Captain Picard, we are embarking on a journey from failure toward success. It's important for us to think about what lies ahead of us. But we need to think honestly about what obstacles we may encounter. We need to lay aside those negative thoughts that might dissuade us from taking the journey.

When I first went to college to become a doctor, I couldn't imagine that it would ever *really* happen. Deep in my heart, I *knew* that I wasn't cut out to be a doctor. I couldn't visualize myself wearing a white doctor's coat and treating patients. I couldn't foresee working with other doctors to diagnose diseases. And I definitely couldn't envision attending four additional years of medical school and two years of residency after college. The only reason I enrolled in pre-med was because I knew that a doctor made a lot of money—a very poor reason to pursue a career for which I was not suited.

When I finally made the decision to become a school teacher, my future became quite clear. I could *easily* imagine myself standing in front of a group of students—explaining to them how to solve complex problems. I could envision sponsoring a club or coaching a team. I could picture myself as a person to whom students could talk about their problems. I knew that my own unique struggles as I transitioned from high school into college could be a benefit to students as they prepared for their own uncertain path toward the future.

STEP THREE: CAST A VISION

As my friend Kary Oberbrunner says,

> *"Life isn't about finding yourself, it's about discovering who God created you to be."*

I had told Russ Keller that I would *never* go back into another high school as long as I lived—closing my mind to a possible future career simply because I didn't like being a student. It took getting kicked out of college and nearly losing my girl-friend to recognize that God had created me to be a teacher. In hindsight, I am amazed at how clearly everything came into sharp focus once I let go of my own ego and opened myself up to an entire set of alternate possibilities that I had resisted since high school.

When I set aside my own stubbornness—I was able to cast a vision. I imagined a future that I believed was achievable—something I had been unable to do as a pre-med student. I was able to create a mental picture of where I could go and what I could be. A revised picture of my future wasn't hard to perceive, and surprisingly, I didn't even realize I was creating it!

> "LIFE ISN'T ABOUT FINDING YOURSELF, IT'S ABOUT DISCOVERING WHO GOD CREATED YOU TO BE."

THE FOUR E'S

A simple four-part process empowered me to create a new future for myself. I call this process "The Four E's": Exonerate, Eliminate, Examine, and Embrace.

EXONERATE

The Merriam-Webster dictionary defines exonerate as "to clear from accusation or blame." To exonerate ourselves means to forgive ourselves for our past mistakes.

This isn't always an easy step. No one *wants* to be the focus of blame. But when we clearly recognize the steps we have taken that have placed ourselves in our current circumstances, it is important to clear ourselves of blame before we begin walking down a different path toward success. Accepting responsibility for our situation is an important first step in exonerating ourselves. Once we have accepted our own fault in a situation, we can begin to forgive ourselves.

Forgiving ourselves is often harder than forgiving another person. When my friend Bill sought forgiveness from his former boss for stealing money, Steve readily forgave him. But the guilt and shame that Bill carried for more than twenty years had become more than he could bear. Even today, though he has been forgiven—exonerated both by Steve and (more importantly) by God—Bill still occasionally struggles with the shame of what he did.

Personally, I carry guilt heavily; it is difficult to forgive myself when I do something wrong, even when I am genuinely remorseful and seek forgiveness. Unfortunately, I carry that same struggle to forgive other people who have wronged me. For example, as a pre-teenager, I experienced physical abuse at the hands of someone I thought was a friend, and I was traumatized for decades. Rather than place the blame where it belonged—on the perpetrator—I blamed myself for allowing the abuse to happen. After seeking professional help, I was finally able to exonerate myself, change my mindset, and move past the pain. But forgiving the abuser has been difficult. My inability to forgive those who have wronged me has caused unfortunate relationship stress and is a character defect that I am working on.

Once I was able to forgive myself for the foolish and irresponsible choices I had made academically, I decided that my next college experience was going to be different. While I didn't necessarily view it as my last chance at professional success, I *did* recognize that my girlfriend was counting on me to make a positive change—to create a possible future that she could get on board with. And I also knew that if I failed academically this time, I might lose my relationship with her.

ELIMINATE

American author, entrepreneur, and motivational speaker Jim Rohn once famously said,

> *You are the average of the five people you spend the most time with.*"

This was certainly true in my case. When I look back at the people I was hanging out with when I got kicked out of college, nearly all of them were high school friends who also had no plan for their future. The only person in my inner circle who really knew what they wanted from life was my girlfriend. And she had made it clear that we weren't going to be together much longer unless I figured out my future.

The second step I needed to take was to eliminate negative influences in my life. It was time for me to make a "decision." The word decision has two Latin roots. The prefix "de-" means "out," and the root word "cis" means "to cut" (think of the word incision—making a cut *into* something). So, making a *decision* is the act of cutting out other choices—eliminating other courses of action.

> YOU ARE THE AVERAGE OF THE FIVE PEOPLE YOU SPEND THE MOST TIME WITH."

When I made the decision to return to college, I was committing a large chunk of my schedule to classes and to study. A natural result of that decision was that I would be seeing my friends less often—I was cutting out the time that I had been spending with them.

Later in my college education, I began student teaching. I still had a part-time job, and I wanted to spend as much time with my girlfriend (who was now my fiancée) as possible, so the time with my friends decreased even further. Eventually, our paths diverged and we all drifted our separate ways.

While some of the negative influences in my life came from the people I spent most of my time with, it would be unfair to place all of the blame on them. The hard truth was that much of the negativity I experienced came from within. I had a negative attitude about everything. I constantly argued with my parents, I refused to go to church, I blew off school, and I held a generally negative view of everything in my life.

When my girlfriend told me to get serious about life, I initially reacted poorly. My default mood in life was negativity, so it made sense that I would react poorly. Although I didn't blow up at her directly, the voices in my head started warring with one another. "Who does she think she is?" "How dare she threaten me like that?" "I don't need her to tell me what to do!"

Once I was able to calm down and rationally look at what she had said, I realized she was not attacking me. She was telling me that she loved me. She *wanted* to be with me. She wanted to marry me. She wanted to have a family with me. Her dream was to be a wife and mom. But she was afraid that her dream of a life with me wouldn't come true if I didn't have my own hopes and dreams for the future. When I looked at my situation through *her* eyes, I recognized that I had the ability to become successful, but I was wasting my God-given talents and gifts on worthless pursuits.

EXAMINE

The decision to return to the same college that had kicked me out was not a given. While I had arrived at the inescapable conclusion that I was not meant to be a doctor, there were still a variety of unexplored avenues down which I could travel.

The third part of the process is to examine the opportunities before you. As I mentioned earlier in the book, I considered a variety of career possibilities during my exile from higher education, including:

- Cruise Ship Janitor: While the thought of living on a cruise ship and traveling around the world sounded sensational, I learned that the job was anything *but* exciting. Cramped living quarters for the staff coupled with very little pay made for a largely miserable work experience according to those who had done it.

- Private Investigator: I actually enrolled in a course and studied to become a private investigator, but I quickly found out that the exciting life portrayed on television did not translate to the actual drudgery of detective work.

- Truck Driver: I got my driver's license to become a truck driver, but the idea of spending many hours a day for weeks on end monotonously driving a truck around the country made me absolutely miserable.

- Soldier: the closest I came to acting on any of these options was when I nearly enlisted in the Air Force. I recognized the only reason I was doing it was because I didn't have anything going on in my life. Also, a friend of mine was about to enlist himself, which was a very bad reason to make a life-altering decision.

I ruled out all of these options and decided that I needed to go back to college. I knew I wasn't cut out to be a doctor, but I gave serious consideration to becoming a surgical technologist. "Surge-techs" are the doctor's assistants in the operating room. They clean and prep the room for surgery, making sure that all of the necessary equipment is present, sterilized, and ready for the doctor's use. They account for all equipment during and after the surgery—making sure that nothing used during the surgery gets left inside an unsuspecting patient. They also clean up the operating room after surgery.

It sounded fascinating, but I feared that it would require many of the same courses that had led me to failure during my first stint in college. I would also have to enroll in a different university that was much further from my home, making the travel time and cost of gas more burdensome.

My second option was to return to Indiana University Northwest, my "not-quite alma mater," the school that had invited me to leave just eighteen months before. Russ Keller told me that I would make a good math or science teacher, and IUN had an excellent education program. I finally decided to stop rebelling against my apparent skills and talents—as well as the wisdom of my high school counselor. I would go back to IUN and become a high school math teacher.

More than thirty years later, I look back and recognize that this is the path I should have chosen from the beginning. My own stubborn pride prevented me from pursuing my natural abilities, and it cost me eighteen months of my life. On the plus side, I now have an awesome story that I can share with my students—many of whom are experiencing the same struggles that I did when I was their age.

If you are lost like I was, I'm sure that you have considered some options for your future—some of them impractical, and some of them very realistic. Often, the most realistic options are the ones we rebel against the most, because they don't seem "exciting enough." The reality is that we have skills, talents, and abilities that are geared toward certain career possibilities, and we can only experience maximum excitement and true fulfillment when we engage in *those* areas. The only things that can come from pursuing a career that we are not cut out for are stress, disappointment, and more failure.

EMBRACE

The fourth part of the process is perhaps the most important. I had to embrace the future I had begun to imagine for myself. To embrace means more than to simply accept a new vision for my life. It is a willing and enthusiastic agreement—a total commitment—to change. A half-hearted effort would not get the job done.

In *The Big Book of Alcoholics Anonymous*, we read: "half measures availed us nothing. We stood at the turning point." This statement summed up my life at the age of twenty. I was at a pivotal moment—a turning point in my life and offering another lukewarm (or half-measured) effort would do no good. I needed to be "all in" if I was going to succeed. In hindsight, I recognize that flunking out of college a second time would likely have led to the dissolution of my engagement and would have had devastating consequences to my own sense of self-worth and, ultimately, to my future.

I embraced the opportunity in front of me. This decision required a mental shift—the need to let go of my internal negativity—which was extremely difficult. I needed to experience some quick, short-term success that would improve my focus and provide a foundation for a positive mindset.

I had to take a reinstatement seminar in order to get back into college. The purpose of the seminar was to help me become better prepared to succeed. The instructor taught us time management skills, study techniques, and a variety of other important life skills that are critical for success as a college student.

Once I was officially reinstated, I retook two courses I had failed previously (one of which was, ironically, a math class). I replaced those two Fs with an A and a B+. My grade point average jumped from a 1.44 to a 2.33 in one semester, removing me from academic probation. I was on my way!

As I started to experience academic success, it became easier to embrace the new path that I was on. I was able to let go of my negativity and more clearly envision a future for my fiancée and me—one that included all the things we both wanted, including marriage, family, and career.

SO, WHAT ABOUT YOU?

As you have been reading, I'm sure you have thought about some of your own failures—mistakes that altered the direction of your life. My deepest hope is that you have been encouraged—that you have come to the realization that we do not need to be defined by our mistakes. We can overcome our past missteps, but first we must change our way of thinking.

What failures have you made you feel defeated? Is it the loss of a relationship? A moral failure? Did you hurt someone (intentionally or unintentionally) and you have been gripped by guilt over your actions? Maybe, like me, you have been emotionally or physically abused, and the trauma of those events has destroyed your sense of self-worth. There are any number of ways that we fail, or have been failed by others, on a daily basis, and it is easy to slip into a defeatist mindset—a mode of thinking where we blame ourselves for everything and see no way out.

It's time to exonerate yourself—to take your first steps toward self-forgiveness. Understandably, that is often easier said than done. Like my friend Bill, you may need to go to someone you have wronged to ask for forgiveness. You might need to seek wisdom from a trusted friend, adviser, or confidant. Maybe you will need to seek professional counseling, like I did. If you don't know Jesus Christ, then you should seek Him out. He freely offers forgiveness and salvation for ALL of our sins.

Whatever your individual situation, it is essential to your future success that you find a way to forgive yourself so that you can move on. Otherwise, you will find yourself trapped in a cycle of self-defeat and despair from which you may be unable to escape on your own.

Once you are able to let go of your past mistakes, you will need to take a hard look at the influences in your life that are helping you to make poor choices. Those influences are often habits or patterns of behavior that distract us from our goals. Unfortunately, those behaviors are often tied to people that we genuinely care about. In my case, it was the friends I hung out with who had no motivation to improve their position in life after high school. It was easy to hang out at a video arcade with them and mindlessly play video games instead of studying or going to classes.

It is critical for you to identify the negative influences in your life—whether they are people, habits, or even addictions that you need to overcome.

ELIMINATE THE NEGATIVE INFLUENCES

In Appendix A, located on page 157, is an exercise that may help you identify some of the negative influences in your life. It's important that you complete this exercise as honestly as possible. This is no time to allow emotions to get in the way! You are at a crossroads—a pivotal moment where you have decided to eliminate those things and people from your life that are holding you back from success.

Once you have completed the negativity elimination exercise, you may need some time to mentally and emotionally process through the results. While bad habits are difficult to change, they rarely have a long term effect on us once they have been broken. When I had to give up playing video games every day because it was a huge waste of my time, I missed them for a little while. But within a couple of weeks, I didn't think about them very much at all. A bad habit is usually something we can overcome mentally. For example, when I recently realized how much time I was wasting (again) on online video games, I immediately deleted the app from all of my electronic devices. I haven't played those games in months, and I rarely think about them anymore.

Addictions are more complicated to eliminate than simple bad habits—particularly if you are addicted to drugs, alcohol, food, sex, gambling, or any of a variety of unhealthy dependencies. To eliminate these, you may need to seek the help of a 12-step program fellowship, a professional counselor, a trusted friend, or a spiritual adviser. It is critical that you not shy away from seeking help. Addictive habits are among the most difficult negative influences in our lives, and they often impact us physically, emotionally, and mentally. But when we overcome them, the sense of victory that we experience is powerful enough to propel us to heights of success that we didn't imagine were ever possible.

My wife started smoking at the age of fourteen and smoked for nearly ten years. The day she found out she was expecting our first child, she quit smoking cold-turkey. While it was not easy for her, the need to protect the health of our unborn son was more important to her than the craving for a cigarette. Eight children and more than thirty years later, she has not touched another cigarette.

Unfortunately, the most difficult decision to make when removing negative influences from our lives surrounds how we deal with negative people. If you are employed at a job where your boss or other co-workers make going to work incredibly stressful, the decision to look for another job is not that tough. It may take time to find a new position, but the decision is actually quite simple. However, there is an emotional component to our relationships with other people that cannot be fixed by just quitting a job.

For instance, if one of the key areas of negativity in your life is a sibling or a parent, you cannot simply "quit" your family—especially if you are still in high school or college. Running away is not the right solution and will only lead to even more stress and negative consequences. You need to find a way to get along with the people with whom you share living space. The good news is that there are some things you *can* do to limit your exposure to the negativity that you experience around your family.

As you identify the negative people in your life, also identify the positive people, those who make you feel good about yourself—the individuals who accept you for who you are, flaws and all, and encourage you to reach for your goals. This might mean that you need to seek out new friends or mentors. If you are in school, you can often find those people in a club or an organization dedicated to a common interest. One of my sons was an English major in college, and he found some of his best and most encouraging friends in his university's English club. My daughter Sarah recently lost a friend who was an extremely negative influence. She often made Sarah feel angry or inferior, and, in hindsight, was not really much of a friend at all. The former friend ended their relationship with a nasty letter, telling Sarah that she had outgrown their friendship and needed to move on.

Sarah met her new best friend Rosalie through a local 4-H club meeting. Rosalie is one of the kindest, most gentle, and generous young women I have ever met. She is a genuine encouragement to Sarah, and is a very positive and stabilizing influence in Sarah's life.

When I was in high school, my relationship with my parents was generally very negative. But when I was fifteen, our church hired a new youth pastor, Steve Buchelt, to revitalize the youth program. Steve infused the high school students in our church with an energy that we had never experienced before. His influence helped me develop better relationships with my parents.

Additionally, Steve built relationships between himself and the youth, the youth and each other, and the youth and the church. We called our youth group "Power Unlimited" (or P.U., for short) and that youth group proceeded to do great things for the cause of Christ in Crown Point, Indiana.

Steve identified a small group of five student leaders (including myself) and he met with us for breakfast at McDonald's every Thursday morning at 6:00 AM before school. We met for prayer, encouragement, mutual accountability, and strategic planning. It was not easy to get up that early every week, but it was worth it! It was an amazing time of connection with my peers—some of whom I did not know very well. I developed new, positive relationships, and those experiences helped me to develop leadership skills that still serve me to this day. Steve wasn't afraid to call us out for our negative behavior, but, even when he admonished us for doing something wrong, he affirmed our value and sense of worth as a child of God.

Over 35 years later, Steve is still one of the most influential people in my life. I don't make a major life decision without asking for his advice, and I am grateful that the positive guidance he has brought into my life has contributed to the success I have experienced—both in ministry and in higher education.

At the end of the activity in Appendix A, you will be asked to identify positive influences in your life: coaches, trainers, teachers, mentors, pastors, bosses, and so on. I would encourage you to reach out to some of those people that you identify and let them know what a positive impact they have had on your life. You will encourage them in ways that you cannot begin to imagine, and you will be inspired to emulate the positive influences in your life as you begin to eliminate those who are having a negative impact on your future.

CHAPTER FIVE

"Faith is taking the first step even when you don't see the entire staircase."

—Martin Luther King

TAKING THE SUCCESS STAIRCASE

G oal achievement is not simply about the destination; it's about the journey. The more challenging the goal, the easier it is to give up along the way. Just as a baby stumbles when they are learning to walk, you will have missteps along the way as you move toward your goals.

This has been hard for me to internalize and overcome. I'm a perfectionist in many ways, and when it comes to taking that first step, I often find myself procrastinating because I'm afraid. If everything isn't "perfect," I don't think that I will do a good job—I'm afraid that I will fail.

STEP FOUR: TAKE THE FIRST STEP

I have found that the best way to achieve a long term goal is to break it into steps—setting mid-range goals along the path toward your ultimate goal and then celebrating those milestones as you achieve them.

At one point in my life, I weighed so much that the doctor's scale could not register how heavy I was. Back in the days before everything was digital, I stepped on the scale at the doctor's office, the nurse slid the metal bar to the right all the way to 350, and the weight indicator didn't move. The nurse looked at me with pity, glanced down at my chart, and said, "We'll just write 350+." This was easily one of the most humiliating experiences of my life. I wanted to cry. The best guess is that I weighed somewhere around 360 pounds. This is the number that I have accepted as my heaviest weight.

WHAT COULD I DO?

I knew that I needed to lose weight. All of the "ideal weight" charts said I should weigh about 200 pounds. But losing 160 pounds was so daunting—the goal was so large, that the thought of even trying made me want to cry (and sometimes I did).

I was 41 years old when my youngest child, Rachael, was born. I knew that I wanted to see this little red-headed, blue-eyed bundle of joy grow up. I wanted to walk her down the aisle on her wedding day. I wanted to experience the full joy of her life. I wanted her to remember her father in real life, not from a photograph. At that time, I weighed 345 pounds.

I set a big goal. I wanted to weigh 225 pounds (I think that the "ideal weight" charts are often unrealistic). I set some mid-range goals. The first was to weigh less than 300 pounds. Although losing 45 pounds seemed like an impossible task, it was a lot easier to think about than losing 120 pounds!

I battled my way down to 300 pounds. The day that the scale hit 299, I was ecstatic. I felt like Rocky Balboa when he ran up the steps of the Philadelphia Museum of Art in the movie *Rocky*. The achievement of a mid-range goal was a huge victory.

When I graduated from high school, I weighed 280 pounds. This has been the weight listed on my driver's license since I was eighteen. It seemed like the next logical goal mid-range goal to pursue. The day that I stepped on the scale and it read 279.4, I was overjoyed. At that moment, I weighed less than I did before high school, before I met my wife, and before I knew most of the important people that shaped my life. I felt renewed!

Once I got below 280, I set a goal of 260 pounds. This milestone had numerical significance for me—once I got below 260 pounds, I would have lost 100 pounds...ONE HUNDRED POUNDS! I never in my life believed that I would lose 100 pounds.

A few weeks ago, I stepped on the scale. It said 259.2. I am officially a big loser, though I am not done!

My next goal is close; I want to weigh 250 pounds. Among his many talents, my friend Steve Buchelt is also a pilot. He flies a small World War II reconnaissance warplane. He has taken many of his friends on flights around northwest Indiana—but not me. The weight limit for his passengers is 250 pounds (did I mention that this is a *small* plane?). Steve has been a friend for over 35 years and has always been an extreme source of encouragement to me. He has reminded me for years that he wants to take me flying with him. Once I get solidly below the 250 pound threshold, Steve will be able to take me for a flight in his World War II "Chipmunk" recon plane—a trip that I will savor with great joy.

After 250, my goal will be the finish line—225 pounds. By breaking my weight loss goal into chunks and celebrating the victories along the way, I am focused, not on the mountain I am climbing, but simply on the next summit I need to reach. And each summit brings me closer to my ultimate goal. And when I reach that goal, I will have lost a whopping 135 pounds—something I could never have done if I focused only on the end result.

Writing this book is another perfect example of the fear-based procrastination that I struggle with. I am a morning person—my most productive time of the day is typically between 5:00 AM and 10:00 AM. If I don't sit down and write during that time frame, I often don't get anything written that day.

In reality, I *could* write at other times during the day. Even if it isn't "perfect," it will still give me a foundation for ideas to flow out during my peak efficiency time. But because I have invented this idea of the "perfect writing environment," I struggle to get words on paper at any other time of the day. Even at this moment, it is after 10:00 AM, and I can feel my attention and focus starting to wane. But I have committed to writing until at least 1:00 PM., trusting that *something* I write during the next couple of hours will make it into the final version of this book!

There is more than one first step that you can take to propel yourself into a new future. All of them involve taking some kind of action—you can't get anything done without initiating some kind of forward movement. There are a variety of actions you can start with.

BELIEVE IN YOUR DREAM

You can't achieve lofty goals if you don't believe that your dream is worth achieving! No one can put in maximum effort for a dream or a goal that they do not believe is worthy of their effort.

In his best-selling book, *Start with Why*, Simon Sinek suggests that people will not gravitate toward *what* you do until they can understand *why* you do it.

So why am I writing this book? It's not in the hopes of making millions of dollars in book sales (although that would be nice!). It's because I was an academic failure. And in more than 30 years of teaching, I have encountered hundreds of other students who are experiencing the same kind of thing I went through when I was 19. They don't know what they want to do with their lives, they have experienced academic failure because of their lack of direction, and their sense of hopelessness.

Every time I waver in writing this book, I am reminded that if I can help just one student get through those same struggles that I experienced when I was in college, writing this book will have been worth it. That's the dream I believe in with all my heart—to help high school and college students succeed.

Do you believe in your dream? Is it worth giving your best efforts to? I hope so. If you don't, it doesn't mean you are a failure. It simply means that you need to find another dream to pursue.

MAKE A PLAN

In his classic leadership book, *The Seven Habits of Highly Effective People*, Steven Covey writes that we must

"begin with the end in mind."

This is the second of his seven habits and it requires us to use our imagination to envision what we want to accomplish or where we want to end up—to see with our mind what we cannot currently see with our eyes.

I try to do this every time I begin a new challenge. I am a tactile planner, so I enjoy the feeling of a pen in my hand

"BEGIN WITH THE END IN MIND."

and a pad of paper on my lap rather than a keyboard under my fingers and a screen in front of my eyes. Whenever I start a new project, I sit down with pen and paper and I write down what I want to accomplish. Once I know what the goal or the destination is, I can then begin to write out the intermediate steps or goals necessary to carry me to my desired result.

EXPECT IT TO BE HARD

Nothing will derail your plans more quickly than setting unrealistic expectations about how much work it will take to make your dreams come true. As Theodore Roosevelt once said,

"Nothing in the world is worth having or worth doing unless it means effort, pain, difficulty... I have never in my life envied a human being who led an easy life. I have envied a great many people who led difficult lives and led them well."

NBA Hall of Famer Kobe Bryant was notorious for his work ethic. Michael Jordan once said that Kobe was the only player he had ever seen who could match his own incredible work ethic. When Kobe was in high school, he would shoot baskets for two hours *before* school to improve his shot. In one NBA game, he played left-handed after injuring his right shoulder earlier in the game.

Kobe once said of himself: "To think of me as a person that's overachieved, that would mean a lot to me. That means I put a lot of work in and squeezed every ounce of juice out of this orange that I could."

While I would never compare my own journey to an NBA superstar, I understand what Kobe means. When I was in school, I was constantly ridiculed for my weight. To have reached a point (in my fifties) where I weigh less than I did when I was seventeen is almost unbelievable to me. I have had to put in a LOT of work over the years to reach my current weight. And even though I am not yet to my final goal, I have a deep understanding of the work it will take for me to eventually get there.

I also have a deep understanding of the hard work it takes to overcome academic failure and achieve success—obtaining not one, but two college degrees. If you are struggling with the same kinds of academic issues, I have good news: you *can* reach your goals. Achieving our dreams is hard. But that's what makes them dreams...and that's what makes them *worth it*.

BREAK IT DOWN

Q: "How do you eat an elephant?"
A: "One bite at a time."

Yes, it's an old joke, but it carries a kernel of truth. When faced with a large task, you *must* approach it one small bite at a time. For example, when I set out to write this book, I started by outlining the steps I wanted to include. Then I organized them into sections. Once that was completed, I broke the sections down into individual chapters. Then I began researching chapter one—which included examples of famous people who had famously failed. I approached each chapter in the same manner. When I first thought about writing a book, I was overwhelmed by the enormity of the task. But by breaking it down into smaller chunks, I was able to focus on the next step instead of all the steps that would follow.*

I did the same thing when I returned to college. As I mentioned in a previous chapter, I re-enrolled in just a couple classes that I had failed and I focused on achieving success for those two classes. If I had thought about the 30-plus classes I would have to take after those first two, I might never have returned to college.

I recently read about a woman who is about to climb Mount Everest for the ninth time—and become the first woman to hold that record. It takes *weeks* to climb Mount Everest. It's not something you can do over a long weekend. There are numerous base camps along the path that hikers stay at—sometimes for days—in order to acclimate themselves to the extreme weather and lack of oxygen at each altitude. While a climber's ultimate goal is to reach the top of the mountain, failing to focus on what he or she is doing *right now* could make that goal elusive and could even prove fatal.

BE ACCOUNTABLE

Once you have broken down your task into a series of steps, it is important to get started immediately and *do something every day*. Accomplishing a goal is like strengthening a muscle: the more you work at it on a consistent basis, the more success you will achieve. You cannot expect to see sustained success if you only work at it when you feel like it. Take a few small

---

* An excellent tool for breaking down your goals into manageable chunks is the Full-Focus Planner© by Michael Hyatt. Read more about the FFP© in Chapter Ten.

steps every day, and you will begin to experience success that you didn't think was possible!

Once you have set your course, telling someone about your plan is a good idea. Being accountable to another person when we set a goal is a great foundation to success—especially when the goal is challenging.

When you choose someone to share your goal, dream, or destination with, you should make sure that they are someone who supports you without reservation and who is not in competition with you for a similar goal. This can be a parent, best friend, clergyman, spouse, or trusted mentor, but you need to make sure that you are willing to take constructive feedback from this person, even if it might be a little painful. Proverbs 27:6a says,

"Faithful are the wounds of a brother..."

This simply means that if someone has our best interests at heart, we can trust that their words are genuine and meant to help us, even if they sting a little bit.

Accountability is a very important action step, but it is not to be taken lightly. If you reveal yourself to the wrong person, their criticisms can be incredibly destructive. There are only a few people in my life that I allow into that kind of close relationship: my wife, my mastermind group, and one or two other close friends in whom I have complete confidence. Other than those few people, I do not share my goals broadly.

"FAITHFUL ARE THE WOUNDS OF A BROTHER..."

One of the biggest mistakes that some people make is to announce their goals on Facebook or some other form of social media. This is a great way to experience an incredibly negative backlash that can be destructive to your self-esteem and ultimately damage any progress toward your goals and dreams.

The internet is a place where everyone perceives a sense of anonymity. This makes it easy for people to troll you and say things that they wouldn't have the courage to say to your face. There is absolutely no upside to sharing something as personal as your deepest goals and aspirations on social media. You will find more naysayers than supporters. And no matter how committed you are to your destination, the negative people will plant unnecessary seeds of doubt that will only spring up as weeds on your path to success.

FIND LIKE-MINDED PEOPLE

One thing that the internet CAN be good for is finding people who have experienced success in the same areas you are seeking to reach. People like Michael Hyatt, Dan Miller, Ray Edwards, Kary Oberbrunner, Kris Pavone, and Cliff Ravenscraft have all experienced high levels of success as speakers, authors, and content providers. Their successes have attracted other people like myself who want to achieve similar goals.

Connecting with these people both online and face-to-face has encouraged and inspired me in ways that I could never have imagined. Whenever I am struggling to push through a barrier in my career, there are so many like-minded people out there who have experienced similar struggles, and they are happy to share their own stories of overcoming adversity.

Comedian Vir Das once said:

"Surround yourself with a bunch of like-minded people, and you'll soak up their habits like a starved sponge..."

Nothing could be more true. When pursuing your goals, surround yourself with like-minded people. You will benefit from their habits, and, believe it or not, *they* will benefit from yours. Remember, you are the average of the five people you spend the most time with.

CHAPTER SIX

"...vision is true north for the soul...a permanent, intuitive compass direction for a human being. Every person inevitably strays from the path...vision brings one back to the true path."

—*Thomas G. Bandy*

"HOUSTON, WE HAVE A PROBLEM"

One of my favorite movies of all time is *Apollo 13*. This movie ranks near the top of my cinematic top ten list for several reasons: the all-star cast includes two of my favorite actors (Tom Hanks and Gary Sinise); it's a true story of heroism; and it's filled with multiple lessons on teamwork, strategic thinking, effective leadership, and the determination to succeed against the greatest of odds.

For those who have not seen the movie, the Apollo 13 mission in April of 1970 had to be aborted when an onboard oxygen tank exploded, severely damaging the spacecraft and making it impossible for the three astronauts to land on the moon. Mission Control at NASA had to find a way to keep the astronauts alive with a limited oxygen supply while at the same time making a plan for the damaged ship to return to earth.

One of the most exciting moments in the movie was when the astronauts had to do a controlled burn of their engines in order to course correct their flight trajectory and get the ship on a proper re-entry path. The angle at which the ship entered the atmosphere on its return to earth had to be 100% accurate. If the ship entered the atmosphere at too steep an angle, the friction of the atmosphere against the capsule would cause so much heat that the heat shield would fail and the astronauts would be burned alive.

But if the angle of re-entry was too shallow, the capsule would skip off the atmosphere, much like a stone skipping across a pond. The capsule would shoot back into space and the astronauts would die a slow, cold death as their oxygen ran out and the ship continued into deep space.

The explosion of the oxygen tank caused a lack of power to the spaceship, so the astronauts were unable to use the onboard computer to fire the engines. They had to do it manually—a nearly impossible task.

I have watched *Apollo 13* at least a dozen times. Even though I know how the movie ends, I still find my heart racing during the engine burn. The course correction is a matter of life and death, and the actors skillfully bring to life the stress of the situation in a very real way.

IT TASTES LIKE CARDBOARD!

In 2009, Domino's Pizza ranked near the bottom of the fast-food industry in customer satisfaction. People complained that their pizza crust "tasted like cardboard"[1] and the sauce "tasted like ketchup."

Then, Domino's suffered a major public relations nightmare when video of two employees who were tampering with pizza orders went viral on YouTube. The employees were fired and arrested for food tampering.

Domino's was a multi-billion-dollar company, but sales were lagging and they knew that they had to make changes, not only because of the complaints about the taste of their pizzas, but also because of the public perception created by the acts of their former employees.

In 2010, Patrick Doyle was hired as the new CEO. Under his leadership, Domino's created a $75-million ad campaign that *admitted* its pizzas weren't that good—making a decision contrary to what any marketing executive would tell a company to do! Then, the company committed to making its pizzas better, and asked former customers to come back and try it.

Domino's also revamped its menu, implemented an online ordering system, and experimented with other sales options, including an online wedding catering registry!

In 2008, before the employee tampering debacle, shares of Domino's pizza stock sold for just $4 on the New York Stock Exchange. As of November 2018, Domino's shares were selling for more than $250 apiece and the stock has risen faster than Amazon, Apple, Facebook, and Google. Domino's took advantage of the lessons they had learned from failure and increased their market share by more than 5,000%!

STEP FIVE: MAKE COURSE CORRECTIONS

Fortunately, the course corrections we need to make in our own lives are rarely matters of life or death or even of a business failing or succeeding. Most of the time, we have the latitude to experiment—to make minor changes in our path without the fear of losing everything.

I failed to make a course correction during my first semester of college. Within a couple of weeks, I knew that medicine was not the right career path for me. But I was afraid of what my friend Betty would say after she gave me all that money to go toward college. I pushed ahead—destined to fail because of my fear of what other people thought and my unwillingness to change direction.

Of course, hindsight is 20/20. I should have withdrawn from my biology class after the second week of the semester. I would have been able to get some of my tuition money back, and I could have focused on the other courses I had enrolled in. I also could have chosen a replacement course that interested me more than biology, and it even might have encouraged me on a different academic path.

Instead, I gave a half-hearted effort, escaped with a D, and enrolled in *another* biology class the next semester. I was behaving like the joke about the lost driver who decides to speed ahead instead of stopping for help at the nearest gas station. When his friend says, "Hey, I think we're lost! We should ask for directions," the driver says, "Yes, we're lost. But we're making great time!"

WHADDYA MEAN WE'RE IN CLEVELAND?

Every time you board an airplane, you expect to exit the airplane at your intended destination. You put your trust in the pilot to fly you directly to where you want to go without any problems. You don't expect to get on a plane bound for Hong Kong and exit the plane in Cleveland. That would be unacceptable!

But what if I told you that a pilot's job is not to get you where you want to go, but instead, it's to make sure you don't end up where you *don't* want to be?

In his book *Flight Plan: The Real Secret of Success,* Brian Tracy explains that, "From the time you take off, [the plane] will be off course 99% of the time. All airplanes are off course 99% of the time. The purpose and role of the pilot...is to continually bring the plane back on course so that it arrives on schedule at its destination."

That's a pretty sobering thought, but it doesn't just apply to airplanes. The second part of Newton's First Law of Motion states that "...an object in motion stays in motion with the same speed and in the same direction *unless acted upon by an unbalanced force*" (emphasis added).

In other words, *anything* in motion—whether it is the universe, a vehicle, or your life—is going to stay on the same path (whether moving towards chaos or success) unless an "unbalanced force" acts to change that trajectory.

No one wakes up one day and decides to become an out-of-work bum with no money and no discernible path toward a successful future. It's a slow descent—one in which no course corrections have been made to prevent you from ending up where you *don't* want to be.

NUMBING THE MIND TO REALITY

For me, it was a slow deterioration into video game addiction. To numb the pain of being kicked out of college, I spent hour after hour in a video arcade—a world where I could forget about the struggles I was having in real life.

Some people find other addictions to numb their mind: drugs, alcohol, gambling, pornography, and shopping are just a few ways that people check out of reality. Sometimes an intervention by friends and family is necessary to help provide a needed course correction. Mine was a mini-intervention, staged by one person—my girlfriend. And with the simple words, "*I don't want to marry a bum,*" I received a cold hard dose of reality. I made a course correction, got back on track, and have achieved a measure of success that I would have never imagined possible when I was nineteen.

YOU ARE THE PILOT

The good news is that *you* get to be the "unbalanced force" that changes the trajectory of your life! You get to be the one who makes the course corrections that will steer you in the right direction. You are the pilot of your life. Just like an airline pilot, you don't have to make dramatic changes all at once to get your life headed back on the right trajectory.

Small changes are sufficient to start moving you in the right direction. Here are a few *small* things you can do to begin making positive course corrections in your personal life:

GET UP EARLIER

Research shows that the most productive people are those who rise and get moving earlier in the morning.[2]

I remember that when I was living the "bum" lifestyle, I would often sleep until noon, drag myself around the house until it was time for work, and then stay up until 2:00-3:00 in the morning. I thought I was enjoying my sleep patterns until I started getting up earlier. I found myself to be far more productive when I woke up no later than 7:00 AM and got things done.

Now that I'm an "old man," I find the same to be true. In fact, I am most productive throughout the day when I am up by 5:30 AM.

Now I know what you're thinking. "That's not a *small* course correction! I sleep until 10:00 every morning and you want me to get up by 5:30? You're nuts!"

You're right, changing your sleep habits from 10:00 AM to 5:30 AM is *not* a small course correction. That would be a little like driving down the highway at seventy mph and then throwing your car into reverse—NOT a good idea!

But instead of going from 10:00 to 5:30, what about making a plan to go from 10:00 to 7:00—and implement the plan over thirty days? That's a change of 180 minutes over the course of a month—just a six minute change each day.

Each night before going to bed, set your alarm clock six minutes earlier than the night before. The change is so subtle that you won't even notice it at first. And by the end of thirty days, you will be getting up three hours earlier than you were the month before!

GO TO BED EARLIER

Obviously, this goes hand in hand with the previous suggestion. If you have been going to bed at 1:00 in the morning, commit to the same three hour change that will get you out of bed earlier—go to bed six minutes earlier each night for thirty days.

It's important that you do both of these small changes together. If you are still going to bed at 1:00 AM and now you are getting up at 7:00 AM, you have lost three hours of sleep—and getting the proper amount of sleep is one of the most important habits that we can instill in ourselves. In fact, sleep deprivation can lead to a number of health problems, including (but not limited to):

- Heart Disease
- Stroke
- Diabetes
- High Blood Pressure
- Depression
- Decreased Sex Drive
- Weight Gain
- Forgetfulness
- Impaired Judgment[3]

EAT A *HEALTHY* BREAKFAST (OR LUNCH OR DINNER)

"Breakfast is the most important meal of the day."

We've all heard that old saying. Some people swear by it, while others think it's silly. And research has produced mixed results on this hotly debated topic.

What is *not* up for debate is the fact that if you *do* eat breakfast, it needs to be healthy. Too many Americans wolf down a bowl of sugary cereal as their first meal of the day, and then they are surprised when they experience a sugar crash a couple of hours later. These sugar crashes lead to less productive performance throughout the day, and in many cases, to eating even more unhealthy (and often sugary) foods.

If you're a cereal junkie, you don't have to give up cereal entirely. Instead, look for healthier cereal alternatives that use whole ingredients. Read food labels and avoid *anything* that includes High Fructose Corn Syrup (HFCS). Also, mix in some protein and healthy fats to your breakfast routine. A handful of chopped walnuts will add both of these to your cereal and provide a delicious crunch as well. Unsweetened coconut flakes are also a tasty addition to any cereal and provide nutritious fats[4] that will help you feel fuller.

Remember, we're trying to make small course corrections right now. There is no need to radically alter your breakfast menu. And if you're not a breakfast eater, you can apply these same principles to lunch or dinner. The most important thing is that you make some small changes in your diet to begin eating a bit more healthily. You will be surprised at how much better you will feel physically, mentally, and even emotionally.

CUT DOWN ON SCREEN TIME

This is a tough one for me. When I was a video game junkie, my screen time was devoted solely to staring at Ms. Pac Man and Donkey Kong. So, when I went back to college, that time was, by necessity, cut way back.

Then came the arrival of the personal computer. As a teacher, I found myself in need of a PC to keep up with the technological changes in education. I use my computer on a daily basis for work. But now, the same games I paid 25 cents to play in the video arcade 30-plus years ago are available at my fingertips for free, and old addictions die hard.

I occasionally find myself being pulled back into the video game world. This isn't a bad thing as long as I keep it in perspective and under control. But that's often easier said than done.

Your screen time may not be devoted to video games, but I daresay that you—like most Americans—are probably addicted to some sort of electronic device that draws your time away from other, more productive activities.

For most people, it's not their computer that takes all their screen time—it's their cell phone. If I had a dollar for every time I have to ask my students to put their phones away during class, I could retire ten years early!

The reality is that too much screen time is not only robbing us of our productivity—it's also affecting our health! According to a 2014 Nielsen report[5], the average adult spends 11 hours per day looking at a screen. Some of the health side effects to excessive screen time may include:

- Vision problems: including eye strain, blurred vision, and headaches.

- Sleep difficulties: the blue light from screens suppresses the production of melatonin, an important hormone in the promotion of healthy sleeping patterns.

- Weight gain: less active time, poorer sleep patterns, and the ads that pop up with tempting (and unhealthy) food options all contribute to adding pounds.[6]

Additionally, research suggests that teens and pre-teens may experience stunted emotional growth, including social awkwardness and a lack of self-confidence as a result of too much screen time. Furthermore, a recent study by the Journal of the

American Medical Association found that teens who reported not engaging in media use at a high frequency had a lower rate of developing ADHD symptoms (4.6 percent) than did teens who had engaged in at least seven activities (9.5 percent). In other words, the risk of developing ADHD symptoms more than doubled with high use of screens.[7]

So the question becomes "how can I cut down on screen time?" Well, before you can cut back, you need to know how much time you are actually spending on your electronic devices.

There are a variety of time-tracking apps available. Many of them are for parents to track their kids' online usage, but that's no reason for you to shy away from using one. After all, you just want to know how much time you are spending online so you can cut back a bit. Find an app that works for you and then use it for a couple of weeks to get a good baseline for how much time you spend online and what you are using your devices for. This will give you a good starting point.

Once you know how much time you are spending online, review, then examine *where* you are spending that time. Is it time well-spent? Or is it mindless surfing without any real purpose? You will have to make some hard decisions about how you are going to make the best use of your time.

Once you have determined your time usage, make a decision to cut back on your online time. I recommend that you try to cut back by 20% over the course of a month. So if you are spending ten hours a day on your device, try to cut back to eight hours a day over the course of thirty days. A two hour reduction is 120 minutes. Spread over thirty days, you are only cutting back four minutes a day. When you apply a small course correction like this, it is much less daunting.

One more thing you should implement that will make screen time reduction easier is to shut off all electronic devices at least an hour before going to bed. As mentioned earlier, the blue light from screens affects melatonin production. Giving your brain at least an hour of screen-free time before lying down to sleep will give your brain the time it needs to reset and be better prepared to sleep.

MINIMIZE YOUR TOXIC FRIENDSHIPS

"Toxic" may seem like a harsh word when it comes to friendships, but we have all had them. Often, they are people who are so overtly negative that we can hardly understand why we were ever friends with them. But friendships that keep us stuck in a rut, even if those friends are not mean, nasty, or generally negative, are also toxic.

An unexpected result of going back to college was that I saw some of my friends less frequently. At the time, this felt like a negative (but necessary) side effect. Looking back, I now realize that this was a benefit to my success.

The friends I saw less were the ones that I hung out with when I was living the bum lifestyle. I saw them almost every night at the arcade or the bowling alley, and we wasted time on things that were not pushing any of us toward better futures.

More than thirty years later, I am not really in contact with the people that I spent my days with at the video arcade. I'm Facebook friends with some of them, but our lives are not connected in any meaningful way. And, in fact, that's the way *most* friendships in our lives will end up.

None of my current close friends are people I knew before the age of 13. I have just a few friends from high school that

I am still close to (including my wife), and I don't have any friends from college that I am still in contact with.

The truth is that friends come into and out of our lives, much like orbiting satellites whose paths converge occasionally. We need to be very careful that our closest friends—the ones in whom we cultivate our deepest relationships—are a positive influence in our lives.

I'm not suggesting that we completely cut people out of our lives "cold turkey." But I am proposing that you consider making a small course correction in who you invest your time with. If you find yourself hanging out with the same group of people on an almost nightly basis, ask yourself some hard questions:

- Are these friends helping me to grow personally?

- Am I becoming more productive in my career aspirations as a result of these relationships?

- Are they adding positive value to my life?

- Do I believe that these are people in whom I can trust completely?

You can also ask these questions about yourself. Are you adding value to their lives? Can they trust *you* completely? Are you helping them to become more productive in their lives?

Chances are high that there are people in your life who you will need to eventually say goodbye to. A small course correction may be to hang out with them a little bit less. If you are getting together with them nearly every night, cut it back to a couple of times per week. Find productive things to fill that time. Take a class, read a book, or start a new hobby. All of these things will move you in a positive direction while helping to distance yourself from some of the toxic people in your life.

PROFESSIONAL COURSE CORRECTIONS

The good news is that all of these course corrections in your personal life will become motivators for the changes in your professional life. I have found, with rare exception, that implementing some (or all) of the aforementioned personal changes works for the majority of people.

The bad news is that I cannot tell you exactly what professional course corrections you need to make. Everyone finds himself or herself in a unique situation. What worked for me will not necessarily work for you. Changing your college major may not be the right decision. Maybe you think it's time to quit your job and pursue your dream career. This may be a good decision or it may not. It all depends on your individual circumstances.

The one thing I know for sure follows from the *first* part of Newton's First Law of Motion: "An object at rest *stays* at rest" (emphasis added).

Human beings thrive on change. We need to be doing *something* if we are to grow. If you are "an object at rest"—if you are not doing anything to move yourself forward and grow—you are going to stay exactly where you are.

Are you where you want to be? If not, then it's time to make some course corrections and grow.

CHAPTER SEVEN

"Remember to celebrate milestones as you prepare for the road ahead."

—*Nelson Mandela*

"ARE WE THERE YET?"

As a father of eight kids, I have often heard, "Are we there yet?" coming from the back of the van on long trips. As children, we have very little sense of time relative to distance. So when Kate and I took the family on a vacation to Florida—an eighteen-hour drive—my younger children started asking if we were "there yet" just a couple of hours into the journey.

Fortunately, my wife and I had foreseen the likely impatience of our children, so we built in breaks—not just to use the restroom, but also to do some sightseeing along the way. We gave the kids plenty of advance notice so that, each time we stopped, it felt a bit like a celebration—another step along the way to our ultimate goal, our beach house on the Gulf Coast.

STEP SIX: CELEBRATE MILESTONES

A milestone was originally a stone that was set next to a road every mile to tell a weary traveler how far he or she had journeyed. These still exist alongside highways today. We commonly refer to them now as mile markers, but they serve the exact same purpose—helping us to keep track of where we are on the road to our destination.

WHY DO WE STOP?

We are hardwired from birth to celebrate milestones. New parents do this all the time. The first time their baby smiles, they take a picture and put it on Instagram. The first time she rolls over, they share the video on Facebook. And when they begin to walk, you would think that their baby is the first child in the whole world to overcome gravity and take a step!

First birthdays, first time riding a bike, first trip to the zoo… these are all milestones that parents celebrate around their children. And as our kids get older, there are more milestones to celebrate: becoming a teenager, learning to drive, graduating from high school, turning eighteen…but eventually, we start to celebrate those milestones more and more infrequently. After the age of 21, birthdays aren't as big of a deal. College graduations aren't celebrated the same way that high school graduations are. We're *expected* to get a job after college.

Until we get married (a milestone that we celebrate with a *huge* party), the milestone celebrations tend to dwindle. Eventually, we have children and start the milestone celebrations for our children—forgetting that we, too, deserve to celebrate the milestone events in our lives.

IDENTIFY YOUR MILESTONES

To achieve your ultimate goal, it is critical that you celebrate milestones along the way. Trying to accomplish a goal in one huge "bite" with no points of celebration along the way is a challenging task. In fact, you are more likely to give up on your goals if you don't celebrate milestones along the way.

When I returned to college, I felt a bit overwhelmed by the goal—obtaining my college degree. My grade point average was at 1.44—barely a D, and I was on academic probation. One more semester with poor grades would have gotten me kicked out of the university permanently.

I had decided to become a teacher, but to get admitted into the education program, my G.P.A. had to be at least 2.5—more than a full letter grade higher. Rather than focus on the college degree, or even on getting into the education program, I decided to focus on just two courses—a theater class and a math class that I had failed during previous semesters. Many universities have programs that will allow you to retake a failed course and replace the F with the new grade—removing the failing grade from your G.P.A. I received a B+ in the theater class and an A in the math class. My G.P.A. rose from 1.44 to 2.33 in one semester.

The student coordinator for the education department was so impressed by my effort and my determination to succeed that he allowed me to enroll in the education program, even though my G.P.A. was still slightly below their normal standards for admission. In one semester, I had reached two milestones—I was no longer on academic probation, and I had been admitted into the education program. If he had not been so kind as to waive the minimum G.P.A. requirement for me, I would have had to wait an entire *year* to reapply.

ANOTHER LONG AND WINDING ACADEMIC ROAD

As I write this, my son Andrew is preparing to get into his car, drive 200 miles south, and start a new career. Today is a bittersweet day for me. I will miss him terribly. But as a family, we are celebrating this milestone with him.

It's been a long and winding road for Andrew—one highlighted by success and pockmarked with failure. When he was just sixteen, Andrew was accepted into the Indiana State Academy for Mathematics, Science, and the Humanities—a magnet high school (based at Ball State University) for only the most elite academic students in the state. He was the only home-schooled student admitted into his class. And when he graduated with academic honors, he was chosen to receive the Outstanding Citizenship Award by the faculty at the Academy.

He received a college scholarship and did very well in his first few semesters at IU Northwest—my alma mater. Then he decided to go to school "downstate" at Indiana University. The residential campus life didn't suit Andrew well, and after one semester, he elected to drop out of school.

He wasn't sure what he wanted to do at that point, so he took a few semesters off—living with some friends and working to pay the bills. Eventually, Andrew moved back home and resumed his college career at IU Northwest...for a semester. Unsatisfied with his current choice of major, and uncertain of what he really wanted to do, he dropped out of school again, taking a job as a cook at a local restaurant to pay his bills.

After another year away from school, Andrew got the itch to finish his degree. Knowing that "fry cook" was not the career he imagined for himself, he decided to return to school a third time—determined to finish his degree. Having a knack for foreign languages, he chose to pursue a major in Spanish and a minor in French.

He returned to IUN and graduated with honors. And today, he is returning to his former high school—The Indiana State Academy for Mathematics, Science, and the Humanities— where he will mentor a new generation of Academy students.

Andrew's ultimate goal is not to be a Student Life Coordinator at the Academy for the rest of his life, but it's an excellent first step in his career. We are celebrating his college graduation and his new job—each of which are milestones along the path to his future goals.

It's also a milestone for Kate and me. As parents, we love our kids and we want to be close to them for as long as possible. But eventually, they need to move out on their own and begin their lives. So we celebrate this milestone for ourselves, our family, and Andrew.

PLAN TO CELEBRATE!

Any goal worth pursuing should make you feel motivated, inspired, and, yes, a little bit frightened. If your goals are too small, they will eventually feel unworthy of your efforts. But when you have Big, Hairy, Audacious Goals (BHAGs), they can only be conquered by breaking them down into smaller steps and then celebrating each smaller victory along the way.

The best way to observe milestone events is to plan a celebration at each step on the journey. These might be public celebrations with friends and family, or they may be private—just between you and a significant other. You may even choose to celebrate your achievement completely on your own... and that's okay too. When I weighed well over 350 pounds, I rejoiced when I stepped on the scale and had dropped below

300 pounds for the first time in a decade. But I was still self-conscious about my weight, so I shared that milestone only with my wife. Now that I am on the threshold of 250 pounds, I can't wait to tell everyone! When I hit that significant milestone, I'll be just 25 pounds shy of my goal—225 pounds! And when I get to 225 pounds, I will shout it from the mountain tops that I lost a total of 135 pounds!!!

You may want to celebrate milestones along your journey in these ways:

- Write a gratitude letter to someone who helped you along the way

- Start a success journal

- Treat yourself to a new piece of clothing, or a book, or something else that you have wanted to purchase

- Go out to dinner with a few of your favorite people

- Take a day off to just relax and revel in your success

- Take a selfie to commemorate the milestone

- Help someone else who is pursuing a similar goal

- Travel! It doesn't have to be a long distance or an exotic locale. Take a day trip

- Revisit the past: take some time to reflect on where you began your journey. It can be very motivating!

However you choose to celebrate, the most important thing is to share your success with those closest to you. They will recognize your hard work, they won't think that you are bragging, and they will be able to celebrate *with* you! Most importantly, your success can be an encouragement to them as they strive to achieve their own goals.

CHAPTER EIGHT

"Put that coffee down. Coffee's for closers..."

—*Blake*

FINISH WHAT YOU START

In the movie *Glengarry Glen Ross*, a team of four real estate salesmen and their supervisor compete to sell undesirable real estate at inflated prices to unsuspecting customers. At one point in the film, Blake (no last name) is sent by the owners of the company to "motivate" the salesmen to increase their sales numbers. He threatens to fire everyone except the two salesmen who sell the most real estate by the end of the week.

Levene, the most senior salesman, has not been closing sales deals, and is distracted by his daughter's chronic illness. As he pours himself a cup of coffee, Blake tells him to put the coffee pot down and utters one of the most iconic quotes in film: "coffee's for closers."

STARTERS AND CLOSERS

I am a huge baseball fan. I'm fascinated by the culture change within the game in the last 40 years.

For example, up until the 1970s, a pitcher was expected to pitch an entire game (called a complete game) whenever possible. He was expected to start the game and *finish what he started*. Relievers—pitchers who came into the game when the starter wasn't throwing well—were typically old starting pitchers who didn't have what it took to go the distance anymore. But then, somebody got the idea that pitchers didn't *need* to finish what they started, and the "closer" was born.

In 1974, Mike Marshall of the Los Angeles Dodgers became the first pitcher to win the Cy Young Award (for most outstanding pitcher) as a relief pitcher: a "closer." The closer is someone who comes in and finishes the game: the person whose sole responsibility is to make sure the task that someone else started has been completed successfully. The starter is no longer expected to go the distance.

By the end of the 1970s, starters were no longer expected to finish their games. But in 1980, Rick Langford of the Oakland A's pitched 28 complete games (including a streak of 22 in a row), a number that had become unheard of in the era of the closer. Langford's manager, Billy Martin, was loudly accused of abusing Langford's arm by letting him pitch so much. The following year (1981), Langford again led the majors in complete games, with eighteen. In 1982, Langford threw fifteen more complete games, but never threw another one again. An injury to his pitching arm forced him out of the game by 1986.

In 2017, the major league leader in complete games threw only five of them. Four other pitchers tied for second place with *two* complete games each.

"So what?" you may ask.

Like many people, I'm a starter. I have been for as long as I can remember. I begin things *all the time*. Often, I get quite far down the road with what I have started. But I don't often finish. I am *not* a closer.

At work, I am often successful at starting a project, moving it down the road for a while, and then passing it off to someone else to finish. I usually suggest that I have done all I can with it and it needs a "fresh pair of eyes" to bring it to completion. Oddly enough, this is usually accepted as a valid reason for passing the project on to someone else.

The truth is that I usually get bored…or fearful.

Take this book as an example.

One of the reasons I was afraid to start writing is that I'm not a closer. And a book is not something that can be handed off to someone else to "finish."

I've not closed the deal on several things. I started a novel about eight years ago. It sits in digital limbo. I can't close the deal. I'm fascinated by sunken ships. Fifteen years ago, I started building a scale model of the Titanic. It's sitting unfinished in its original box. I can't close the deal. I have lost 100 pounds. I am stuck. I need to lose another 35. I can't close the deal.

I could ask someone to finish the model or write the novel… but I can't have someone else write this book or lose the weight.

Being a starter is exciting. When we first begin a project, the newness of what we are hoping to accomplish energizes us. We race ahead, ideas pouring from our mind faster than we can get our thoughts out on paper.

But after a while, it gets more complicated. The freshness of a new adventure begins to wane. The ideas don't flow as quickly and easily. We start to get bogged down in the details. It becomes less fun. And we find ourselves struggling to persist. Often, we talk ourselves into giving up: "This isn't as good of an idea as I originally thought," or "No one is really going to be interested in what I am creating."

When it comes to writing this book, I have experienced some of those same feelings. And for a while, I felt like I had a perfectly good reason for wanting to quit writing and give up.

WHEN LIFE GIVES YOU LEMONS...

In the fall of 2017, I came down with bronchitis, which wasn't uncommon for me. I often get a cold or minor cough at least once a year when the seasons change. I figured that it would last for a couple of weeks as usual and then I would be fine.

Weeks turned into months, and I finally went to see the doctor, who gave me an antibiotic. After the round of antibiotics, the bronchitis went away, just in time to celebrate Christmas. But shortly after Christmas, the bronchitis returned with a vengeance, accompanied by chronic fatigue. I found myself with the kind of exhaustion where I could sleep for 8-9 hours at night, but when I woke up, I felt like I hadn't slept at all.

I found it harder and harder to concentrate. It became difficult to teach my classes effectively. And when I would return to my office, I often found myself falling asleep—taking naps between classes. Something was wrong, and I didn't know what it was.

My friend Donna, who is a medical professional, noticed the change in my personality—which had been brought about by the chronic fatigue.

"You need to go to the doctor and get a blood test," Donna said. "You are exhibiting symptoms of Lyme disease." Lyme is an infectious disease that is spread by the bite of the deer tick. Symptoms of Lyme can include rashes, fever, achy or swollen joints, headaches, dizziness, memory issues, difficulty concentrating, and chronic fatigue.

I had been bitten by a tick the previous summer, but I had never experienced the rash that usually comes with a tick bite, so I completely forgot about it. When Donna told me about Lyme, I remembered the tick bite and took her advice seriously, as she has suffered from chronic Lyme for almost two decades.

I scheduled a check-up with my doctor, and he ordered the usual round of blood tests. When I asked him if I could also be tested for Lyme, he agreed, but I could tell by his reaction that he didn't think it was necessary. Although Lyme is more common in the Midwest than it once was, it was still fairly rare. A few days later, I got a phone call from one very surprised doctor—my blood test had come back positive for Lyme disease, and he wanted to see me right away.

"Wow, this is surprising," said the doctor, as he walked into the examination room. "We just don't see this a lot. We're going to do whatever we can to help you get better."

His words were reassuring, but as I investigated more, I came to realize that there were very few doctors in my area who knew much about Lyme disease. There were also widely varying opinions on how to treat Lyme. Traditional medical doctors suggest massive doses of multiple antibiotics, while naturopathic doctors treat Lyme through changes in diet and lifestyle.

Needless to say, my head was swimming from all of the information about my newly discovered disease. The last thing I wanted to think about was finishing this book. I put it on the shelf for a couple of months to focus on my health.

MAKE LEMONADE?

It was easy to rationalize away my need to finish writing this book. "I'm too tired," or "I'm sick—I need to focus on getting healthy," or "I can't concentrate—how the heck am I supposed to write this book anyway?" Frankly, the most common reason for not writing has been that I just feel sorry for myself. I have this chronic, permanent disease that makes *everything* more difficult. What point is there in bothering to write a book?

In the back of my head, I knew that I *had* to write and publish this book for several reasons. And I believe that these reasons apply to everyone at some level, whether you are dealing with a chronic illness or not:

1. **Coffee's for Closers:** As I write this, my trusty cup of coffee sits nearby. I love my coffee. And I want to be known as a closer. I have often struggled to complete important projects. I refuse to let this book join the long list of projects that sit on the shelf, never to see the light of day. It's a point of personal pleasure and pride that I have persevered to get this book published.

2. **I Have Something to Share:** My experience as a college flunk-out is an important example to share with others who are struggling with their own failures. So

many other students have grappled with the same issue of academic failure, and my experience can provide valuable insight for those who want to course correct.

I have often said that if my story had happened to someone else, I would find it to be inspiring. So why can't I find it inspirational just because it happened to me? Negative self-talk, that's why.

3. **God Told Me To:** I have felt prompted by God to share my story of success for decades, and I have rarely followed through on that prompting. In reality, when God tells us to do something and we choose not to do it, that's disobedience. I don't want to be disobedient to God. For me, finishing this book is simply about obeying God.

4. **When Life Gives You Lyme:** I have spent the past few months wallowing in self-pity. But the reality is that this disease will only keep me down if I let it. Lyme disease is just one more challenge for me to overcome. And since this book is about overcoming our challenges, it would be silly for me to shy away from another opportunity to experience success.

5. **Giving Myself a Gift:** The subtitle of Jon Acuff's book *Finish* is "Give Yourself the Gift of Done." What a profound concept. Finishing something *is* a gift—a gift to yourself. When I finished college, I received the gift of a diploma, which gave me the gift of a job as a high school teacher. When I finished my

> "WRITE EVERY DAY AND FINISH WHAT YOU START."

Master's Degree, I received another diploma, which gave me the gift of a university teaching position. And of course, when I finished being a bum, it gave me the gift of a wife, and eventually a beautiful family.

Ernest Hemingway once said that his secret to success as an author was to

"Write every day and finish what you start."

That's easier said than done, but it's a great place to begin. Take Hemingway's quote, substitute your *own* activity in place of the word "write," and say it aloud. Then ask yourself the following questions:

- Am I a starter?

- Am I getting tired?

- Am I looking for a closer?

What have you started that you just can't finish?

Is it high school or college? Is it a home improvement project that you keep dragging your feet on? Is it a relationship that needs to end but you don't know how to do it?

Whatever it is for you, it's time to face your circumstances, accept responsibility, examine your opportunities, cast your vision, take the first step, make course corrections along the way, celebrate the milestones...

And Finish.

PART THREE: SUCCESS

"There is no secret to success. It is the result of preparation, hard work, and learning from failure."

—*General Colin Powell*

CHAPTER NINE

"I have learned that success is to be measured not so much by the position that one has reached in life as by the obstacles which he has had to overcome while trying to succeed."

—*Booker T. Washington*

SUCCEEDING IN COLLEGE

The transition to college—whether it is directly from high school, from the military, or from the workplace—can be difficult. The expectations placed upon you are different, the responsibility for getting things done is exclusively yours, and the results you achieve reflect solely on you.

I was completely clueless about what to expect when I decided to go to college. However, my pride would not let me admit to anyone how naïve I was. Because Betty had given me $3,000, I walked into an academic adviser's office at IU Northwest and boldly declared that I was going to become a medical doctor.

The academic adviser seemed somewhat bored and not really interested in me as an individual. I was just another person in the long line of incoming freshmen that were lined up in his lobby. He rattled through a list of recommended courses for pre-med students, put together my schedule, and sent me out the door. Little did I realize that just three semesters later, I would be gone because of my bad grades.

KNOW YOUR WHY

Now that I am an instructor at the same college, one of the most personally rewarding roles for me has been as an academic adviser for incoming freshmen.

I have met with dozens (if not hundreds) of students who aren't sure what to do when they first come to college. They may have attended the orientation, been given all of the campus tours, and read all of the brochures. But they are hung up on one fundamental problem: they don't know what they want to major in.

They might have no clue what they want to do with the rest of their lives. They might have some vague idea, but they aren't sure what the best degree is for them to pursue. But they DO know one thing—they want ME to help them figure it all out.

What I have learned from interviews with countless students is that many of them don't even know for sure WHY they are starting college. Some of them are doing it because they feel pressured by their parents. Others enroll because they have a vague notion that it is the best way for them to get a good job in the future. But very few students walk into my office with the confidence that they know exactly why they are in college and what they plan to get from it.

While I never try to talk someone out of enrolling in college, I do often ask them probing questions to determine their plans for the future. If a student is feeling uncertain about whether college is right for them, I try to steer them toward courses and opportunities that will ease them gently into the college experience. My desire is that they will be able to determine after just one semester whether college is the right avenue for them. If it isn't, then that semester of college will teach them a valuable lesson—that college is not the right choice for them.

While this might seem odd to hear from a college instructor, I am not naïve enough to think that *everyone* should go to college. I don't think that everyone should enlist in the military or go to a trade school, so why should I believe that everyone should go to college?

Having said that, the rest of this chapter is dedicated to those individuals who have decided that college is the right path for them. Hopefully, these tips, tricks, and practical suggestions will help those of you who are future college students to thrive in your university experience.

FOUR TIPS FOR NEW COLLEGE STUDENTS

RELAX: There is good news! You don't have to know what you are going to do for the rest of your life when you are eighteen years old. Too often, students will come to me in a panic, feeling completely overwhelmed by a schedule of classes with hundreds (or thousands) of courses, and having absolutely no idea which ones to take. They fear that if they don't declare a major right away, they will somehow fall behind. And if they declare the "wrong" major, they will screw up the rest of their life.

More than one-third of all college students change their majors at least once during their college careers. Many students change their majors two or three times before they settle on their collegiate objective. There is absolutely nothing wrong with that! In fact, the majority of courses taken during the first two years of college will fit into *any* degree program. If you take a social work class but then decide that becoming a social worker is not for you, that course will meet an elective requirement in another degree. The same is true with nearly all college courses.

BE FLEXIBILE: This isn't high school. You don't have to take algebra as a freshman, health as a sophomore, U.S. history as a junior, and government and economics as a senior. In fact, you may not need to take any of those classes ever again. And if you DO need to take them, you can probably take them at any time during your college career. You get to decide when to enroll in them, and, in many cases, you get to choose your professor!

HAVE FUN: As an academic adviser, I have found that one of the best ways to help students become acclimated to the university is to try to make their first semester as stress-free and (dare I say it?) FUN as possible. That means finding courses that the student will enjoy. Of course, there are some general education courses that need to be taken early in a college career—Elementary Composition, for example. But there are also opportunities to explore new and interesting classes.

Whenever I meet with a new student for advising, the first question I ask them is this: "What classes did you enjoy in high school?" Once I tap into a student's own interests, I am able to help them craft a schedule that will include at least one or two classes that they won't dread going to on the first day of school.

That intimidating schedule of classes actually becomes a bountiful menu of options—a buffet from which you can select. And just like any buffet, if you try something that you don't like, you can try something else instead. There are always going to be a few classes that you won't enjoy. But if you intermix them in your schedule with those that you do like, it will make your college experience much more enjoyable.

MAKE FRIENDS: One of the best way to plug into college is to find a campus club that interests you. Large residential campuses have hundreds of different clubs and organizations, ranging from religion, athletics, and hobby clubs to social awareness, entrepreneurial, and cultural organizations. Even smaller (and non-residential) campuses will have numerous social clubs and organizations to explore (IU Northwest has more than fifty clubs to choose from). This is a great networking opportunity that also has the potential to clarify a possible career path. And one of the great things about a club is that if you decide you don't like it, you can just drop it and try something else. Usually, you don't have to pay for it (like you do for classes), so there is no risk in exploring a variety of clubs to find the one(s) that best fits your interests.

WHAT DO MY PROFESSORS EXPECT?

Most professors have very reasonable expectations from their students—especially brand-new college freshmen.

I ask my students to follow just five general rules. I call them "The Five P's." Any student who follows them will not only get along well with me in my class, but they will also receive the added benefit of better success in the course, which translates to a higher grade.

BE PRESENT: I expect students to be present. Make sure that you attend each and every class. Sometimes, life might get in the way—a flat tire, an unexpected medical emergency, and so forth. I understand that. But these should be the *exception*, not the rule. Do not schedule medical appointments that conflict with your classes. This is a very frustrating issue for professors. Students should not miss a class and then expect the professor to re-teach them the material at a later date.

Students need to be mentally present as well. Do not do homework or read a book for another course while sitting in my class…do not fall asleep in my class…do not sit and talk to others around you (unless it is an assigned group discussion).

BE PROMPT: I expect my students to be prompt to class. If my class starts at 8:00 AM, do not walk in at 8:05 or 8:15… or 8:30! I'm flexible during the first week when students are still trying to get used to their schedule. The parking lot is often more full than students will expect, so I cut some slack during the first week. But by the second week, I expect that my students will be on time. And, by the way, if you like to stay up late and sleep in on most mornings, then you should NOT schedule yourself for an 8:00 AM class!

BE PREPARED: Come to class with the previously assigned material completed. If homework problems were assigned, make sure you completed them or at least attempted them. Many professors will allow you to ask questions over previously assigned work. If there was a reading assignment, make sure to have read the necessary material so that you can discuss it intelligently. And if you have any questions about the structure of the course, make sure to read your syllabus first. Asking the professor a question that is answered in the syllabus demonstrates that you did not adequately prepare for class.

PARTICIPATE: Nothing delights a professor more than when students in the classroom engage in discussion. If you have come to class prepared, then you will be able to offer your insights on a reading assignment or ask questions about the homework.

Research shows that for every one student who asks a question in class, there are 7-10 other students who had the same (or a similar) question, but they were afraid to ask it. When you participate, other students will look to you as a leader, and they will begin to participate on their own.

PUT: This final "P" has become an important addition to my list over the past few years...it stands for PUT YOUR PHONE AWAY!!!

This has become a large problem in classrooms over the past decade. The overwhelming "need" for students to be in constant communication with everyone at all times has made the job of the college professor much more difficult. Cell phone chirps, people leaving class to answer their phones, and the distraction caused by students texting while the professor is teaching merge to create a chaotic learning environment—one that is not conducive to student success. You (or your parents or the government) are paying too much money for you to sit in a class and not pay attention. You owe it to yourself to turn off the phone and tune in to what is being taught.

By following "The Five P's," you will give yourself an academic boost that will reflect itself in higher grades, a higher G.P.A., the potential for scholarships, and eventually, a boost as you travel along your career path. And I know for a fact that you will have a much better relationship with your professors.

OVERCOMING FIRST DAY JITTERS

It's common to be nervous on your first day of college. You don't know what to expect. You're worried about your professors' expectations. These are common apprehensions for most students.

Over the years, I have recognized a pattern to the disorganization and lack of preparedness that often accompanies the first week of classes. So, here are four things that you should bring to class in order to start off the school year on the right foot:

INSTRUCTOR PREPARED INFORMATION: Nearly all classes have some kind of online classroom management system that will allow you to communicate with your professors, download a syllabus, and verify any needed materials prior to the first day of class. Most professors will have this material posted online about a week prior to the first day of class. If you are unable to locate this type of content, feel free to reach out to the professor via email during the week before classes begin to ask about how to obtain a course syllabus.

WRITING MATERIALS: I am still surprised by the number of students who come to class on the first day without pens or pencils, notebooks, laptops, or any other note-taking tools. Most professors will start teaching on day one. Finding yourself without a way to take notes is a great plan if you are trying to set yourself up for failure.

TEXTBOOKS: This is a big one for many instructors, including me. As a math teacher, I rely on the book heavily from the first day of class for delivering content. With the wealth of textbook access available through the campus bookstore or from online retailers like Amazon or textbook rental companies like www.chegg.com, www.slugbooks.com, and www.dealoz.com, there is virtually no reason for coming to class on the first day without your textbook. The old excuse that "I'm still waiting on financial aid" has also been handled on many campuses (including my own) with an ID card that will allow you to purchase books ahead of receiving financial aid, and then deduct the book prices from the aid check once it arrives to your campus.

A POSITIVE ATTITUDE: Hey, you're in college, right? Embrace it with a positive attitude! Come to class with an expectation that you are beginning a new and exciting chapter in your life. Your professors are there to help you, there are new friends to meet, new experiences to enjoy, and new challenges to face. It's perfectly reasonable to miss the comfort and familiarity of your previous experiences, whether you are coming from high school, the workforce, or if you are an adult who is attending college for the very first time. Life is about change and growth. You are embarking on a path that will stretch you in ways you did not know were possible. Enjoy the ride!

There are also a couple of things that you should NOT bring to class on the first day—or on any day, for that matter. Each professor may have different opinions on this, but in general, here are two things you need to leave at home when you come to class.

CELL PHONES WITH *ACTIVE* RINGTONES: I'm not telling you to leave your cell phone at home. But what I AM telling you is to shut off your ring tones in class. Nothing is more distracting to a professor or to fellow classmates than when a cell phone goes off loudly in the middle of a class. Every phone provides you with the ability to set it to silent (or at the very least, to vibrate). Please silence your cell phones when you come to class. You do it in the movie theaters. Chances are very good that the content you are going to receive from your professor is *at least* as valuable as the content you received from the last movie you watched.

EXCUSES: I'm usually a little more forgiving on the first day when it comes to certain excuses. "I couldn't find a parking spot," "I had to park two blocks away," or "I didn't expect traffic to be so heavy" are frequent first day excuses that I accept as valid. There *is* an element of the unknown in coming to the university for the first time, and I understand that. But after the first week or so, those excuses no longer ring true. Other excuses that don't work for me are, "I overslept," (then why did you sign up for my *8:00 AM* class?), "I'm going to be fifteen minutes late every week because I have to drop my wife off at work on my way to school," (you should probably sign up for a different section of this course so that you can attend the whole class!), or (insert your own excuse here.)

This might make me sound like a mean and intimidating professor, but I actually enjoy teaching my students very much! I simply take my responsibility for your education very seriously. I want you to succeed, and I will do everything within my power to make your success the most likely outcome in my class. I firmly believe that every professor should be equally committed to your success. Don't you?

WHAT IF I HAVE TO MISS CLASS?

The freedom that comes with moving from high school to college is exciting. No longer do we have mom and dad nagging us to get out of bed and get ready for school. No longer do we get "sent to the principal's office" when we act up in class. And no longer do we have to wait for a bell to ring, telling us that it's time to shuffle from classroom to classroom, with only five minutes to get there before another bell signals that we are tardy. We can hang out in the cafeteria with our friends for as long as we want.

But that freedom comes with a load of responsibility that many students find themselves unprepared to handle. It's so easy to roll over and hit the snooze button instead of getting up and getting to that 8:00 AM class. Your professor in a lecture class of 200 students isn't likely to notice if you choose to play football in the quad instead of coming to his or her class. And when your friends in the cafeteria are deep into a debate as to whether Ironman is a *super*hero or merely a hero in a metal suit, your choice to forgo class so that you can engage in the debate will likely go unnoticed by everyone except you.

The reasons for missing class are not always sound, but the fact is that you will have to miss class occasionally. It's important that you do everything in your power to minimize missed classes. But what should you do when an unavoidable conflict arises? Here are three tips for making your life a lot easier when you have to miss a class:

COMMUNICATE: A short e-mail to your professor simply stating that you cannot make it to class will show the professor that you are serious about his/her course. By calling attention to your absence, you are telling them that your education is important to you, and that nonattendance will not be habitual. It demonstrates a level of respect to the professor that will go a long way toward making the class more enjoyable. As a college instructor for more than 25 years, I can tell you that I view the students who let me know when they have to miss an occasional class more favorably than those who simply don't show up without any notice.

CONFIRM: Tell your professor the reason for your absence. If you have a doctor's appointment or other unavoidable conflict, show them a note with the date and time of the conflict that corresponds with their class. If you get a flat tire or are in an accident, use your cell phone to take a picture of the problem.

You don't have to go into detail about your situation. But by validating your circumstances, you are developing trust with your professor while again reinforcing the fact that you value their class and that you are taking responsibility for your own education.

COMMUNITY: Quickly develop relationships in your classes so that when you do have to miss a class, you can connect with another student to get notes, learn of any important announcements, and find out what other key information you may have missed. It is not unusual for a professor to make additions to the classroom syllabus on the fly, like omitting a reading, revising a set of problems, or changing the due date on an assignment. You are still responsible for the material, even if you are not in class to hear of the changes yourself. Having "study buddies" in each class is vital to your college success.

By following these three simple steps, you will go a long way toward establishing success in your college career. You will develop positive relationships and earn the respect of your professors and fellow students. And, most importantly, you will establish positive, character-building habits that will follow you into your post-graduate career.

PROFESSORS ARE HUMAN, TOO

It can be easy to forget that your professors are people, just like you. This concept seems foreign to many students. To a college freshman, professors sometimes seem iconic, untouchable, and almost godlike in their power, authority, and influence over the destiny of their students.

Don't be afraid to talk to your professor when life knocks you down and you are having trouble getting back up. Sickness and death are a part of life. When your life is rocked by the loss of someone close to you, let your professor know your circumstances. Chances are very good that they understand exactly what you are dealing with. Share the situation and ask them how you can best work through the loss while not falling behind in your studies.

Let me step down off the pedestal that some of my students have placed me on. Let me pull back the curtain and reveal something that may take you by surprise—something that will prove I am a person just like you. Granted, I am a person who has more life and educational experience than you, but a person who still deals with the same ebbs and flows of life that you deal with every day.

SOMETIMES, LIFE GETS IN THE WAY

In 2015, I lost my father unexpectedly, just a week before the start of summer classes. I was scheduled to teach two condensed courses, squeezing sixteen weeks of content into four weeks. I hadn't taught one of the classes in a few years, so I needed to refresh myself on the material, restructure the class to fit into a four-week time frame, and prepare all of the tests and quizzes. At the same time, I was grieving the death of my father, settling the details of his estate, and comforting my young children who were dealing with the loss of their grandpa. It was an extremely difficult time.

Honestly, I did not do my best teaching during those four weeks. I was mentally distracted. I was emotionally exhausted. My heart wasn't completely invested in what I was doing, but I had to press ahead. During one class, I was struggling to focus, and I made a few computational errors on the board. Some of my students appeared frustrated by my simple mathematical errors. Finally, I put down the chalk, turned to my class, and told them what I was dealing with. I apologized for my lack of focus and explained to them that I was distracted by the recent death of my father. The irritation that I had seen in some of their faces turned to compassion and understanding when they realized why I was stressed. I relaxed, took a deep breath, and continued with the lesson.

After class, a couple of students came forward and expressed their condolences. Students who had been reluctant or nervous to approach me initially were able to identify with my pain and connect with me, not as their professor, but as just another person who was dealing with loss.

My father's death was a reminder to me as well about how difficult it can be for a student to navigate their way through school when they are dealing with tragedy or loss.

If you find yourself in a similar place—a situation where life has knocked you down and you are having trouble getting back up, meet with your professors as soon as possible. Explain the situation to them. Ask them these three questions:

1. What can I do to avoid falling behind?

2. Can I make up any work that I miss?

3. What resources can I access to help me catch up with anything that I miss?

When you approach your professors directly and honestly, you will be surprised by their compassion and understanding.

AVOID CRAMMING FOR EXAMS

When I was a college student, my inclination when I was overwhelmed with my coursework was to ignore the problem. I figured that I could "wing it," whether it was a test, a speech, or a term paper. Waiting until the last minute to let the pressure drive me to completion became a way of life…a very unsuccessful way of life.

The notion that "cramming for the exam" is the best way to prepare has got to go away. It doesn't work! In a recent study at UCLA, "cramming for a test or plowing through a pile of homework is actually counterproductive." A student who sacrifices sleep for study time is likely to have more academic problems the following day than a student who prepares in a more regulated fashion and gets plenty of sleep.

Here are three tips for better study habits that will help you to avoid cramming and provide better long term academic success:

DISCOVER YOUR INNER CLOCK "SWEET SPOT": The time of day when you are most alert and energized is the best time to study. As I mentioned previously, I am a morning person. My most productive time of day is usually between 5:00 and 9:00 in the morning. One of my friends is a lawyer. He doesn't even get out of bed until 9:00 most mornings, and will often work until 1:00 in the morning. He finds that he is most productive after 10:00 at night. You should also take this into consideration when scheduling your classes.

As an academic adviser, one of my first questions to incoming freshmen is, "Are you a morning person, an afternoon person, or a night owl?" I teach my first class of the day at 8:00 AM. The last thing I want in my early morning class is a group of students who can barely keep their eyes open! If a student tells me that they hate getting up early, I usually recommend that they don't start their class schedule until at least 10:00. In one case, I had a student who slept in most mornings until 10, so I started her schedule at 11:30.

TAKE COMMAND OF YOUR WEEKLY SCHEDULE: Each Sunday night, I like to sit down with my calendar and look at my schedule for the week ahead. I note when I have classes, office hours, scheduled meetings, upcoming events, and so forth. I schedule time for personal development (exercise, reading, and spiritual renewal), family time, and professional opportunities.

As a college student, it is vital that you take command of your own schedule. It is too inviting to allow the demands of your peers, employer, and even parents to dictate your calendar. You need to schedule study times into your week. Pre-decide when those study times are, and don't let other outside influences affect those times. There are only 168 hours in a week, and you should be spending at least 56 of them renewing yourself with effective sleep habits. So that means you only have 112 hours in a week to accomplish all of your other goals. Time is a precious commodity: it is the only commodity that everyone has in common. From the poorest person in the world to Bill Gates, founder of Microsoft, we all have the same amount of time allocated to us. Are you going to let someone else tell you how to use that time?

PREPARE AS YOU GO: Some instructors will allow you to use some prepared notes when you take an exam. Personally, I allow my math students to use a sheet of notes on which they can write any examples, formulas, or definitions that they feel will help them. As I teach, I will tell them about good examples or important formulas for their "help sheet."

Unfortunately, I find that many of my students seemingly wait until the night before (or the morning of) the test to scribble down any last minute notes that they think might help. This is equivalent to cramming and is the least effective way to prepare. Instead, you should be taking good notes and preparing your help sheet during your instructor's lectures.

TEST-TAKING TIPS

If you prepare effectively for an exam, then you should be in good shape for whatever pops up. But there are still some good things you can do in order to maximize your chances for success.

ARRIVE EARLY: This will allow you to take a deep breath, prepare all of your test-taking materials, and focus. Rushing in late during an exam will heighten your anxiety and make it more difficult to get to a place of mental calm where you can concentrate.

SCAN THE ENTIRE TEST BEFORE STARTING: The material that you are most prepared for may not be in the first few questions of the test. If you find something on the last page of the test that you know really well, do that problem first. Knock out some early "victories" on the test. It will give you confidence and help you to relax for the rest of the test.

READ THE INSTRUCTIONS FOR EACH QUESTION CAREFULLY: As an instructor, there is nothing more frustrating to me (and to the student) than taking away a point or two because the answer is correct but not in the proper format. For example, if a math question asks for the solution to the area of a rectangle *using proper notation*, and the answer is 64 ft^2, then 64 is not a correctly formatted answer. In my class, that would cost one point. Make sure you know how the professor wants the answer to appear. And if you are not sure, *ask*.

DOUBLE-CHECK YOUR ANSWERS: If you get done before the class time expires, take a few minutes to review the exam— especially any answers that you weren't sure of. On an essay or written exam, spot check for spelling or grammar errors. On a math test, make sure your computations are correct.

ASK THE PROFESSOR: If you are unclear about a particular question, don't be afraid to ask the professor for clarity. Professors *want* you to succeed. As long as you aren't asking them a question like, "Is this answer right?" they are more often than not glad to help clarify anything that seems muddy to you.

LET IT GO: Once you have turned in the exam, there is nothing more you can do to change it. Let go of any stress you might have about the exam and move on. Take several slow, deep breaths or do some light stretches to ease the tension. Dwelling on the results of a test that you can no longer change is fruitless, and it could affect your ability to focus on your next class.

USE YOUR PROFESSORS' OFFICE HOURS

Every professor has a set aside period of time during the week called "Office Hours." This time is for students to come by for help on an assignment, to clarify the lesson, or to seek advice about how to maximize classroom success.

I tell all of my students that this is THEIR time. They should not be afraid to come and talk to me or ask for help. That's what office hours are for. And yet, invariably, any students who do come to see me peek their head into my office and meekly say, "I'm sorry to bother you, but can I ask you a question?"

Let me tell you a little secret...

YOU'RE NOT BOTHERING ME!

In fact, if I didn't have students, I wouldn't have a job! So, I am happy to help my students when they come by my office. And nearly every other professor I talk to says the same thing. We LIKE to help our students.

But here's the thing: I'm not going to sit at my desk with my hands folded and stare at the wall until a student comes in for help. So, when a student comes to see me during office hours, I *am* usually working on something. I might be writing a test, or grading some papers, or doing some research.

But my students are my number one priority—especially during office hours! So when you peek your head into my office, I might look busy. But whatever I am working on takes a backseat to the needs of my students during office hours.

Now, the flipside is that sometimes we might be working in our office during a time that is not designated for office hours. For example, if I have posted office hours from 1:00 – 4:00 PM on Tuesdays and Thursdays, and a student comes by to see me at 10:00 on a Tuesday morning, I *might* not be able to help them at that moment. I may be finishing an exam for my afternoon class or preparing a report for my department chair, or a number of other things.

If I can take a couple of minutes at that moment to help, I will. But if not, I will gently say, "You know what, I can't help you right now, but can you come back at 1:00 (or whatever time is mutually convenient)? I would be happy to work with you then."

The important thing for students to understand is that we want to help them succeed. They need to be bold enough to come by and seek the help they need. And the best time to do that is during your professors' posted office hours.

CULTIVATE PROFESSOR RELATIONSHIPS

One of the best things you can do to achieve academic success is to develop positive relationships with your professors. This can be difficult at a college where there are 300 or more students crammed into a lecture hall. But if you use their office hours to seek additional help, they will get to know you and appreciate your initiative.

Once you have settled on a major, this is an even more important key to your academic success. The professors in your major are going to be the ones that you have for multiple classes. These professors will be connected professionally to people and organizations outside the university. They will be your best sources for letters of recommendation, overseas study opportunities, and potential internships.

It's important for you to shine in the eyes of your professors, because there are many other students who are competing with you for those same opportunities. While a professor can write a dozen letters of recommendation for his students, there may only be one internship opportunity, and all 12 of those students are competing for the same position. What can you do to elevate yourself in the eyes of your professor so that when he or she writes *your* letter of recommendation, it stands out above the others?

DON'T PASS UP FREE POINTS!

Once, I gave all of my students a chance to earn some extra credit points to kick off the semester. As a math instructor, I know that my classes are intimidating to some, so I tried to take the edge off my students' stress level by asking them to complete a simple writing assignment. It was SO simple that—other than their name—they only had to write 5 (yes, I said FIVE) words on a piece of paper and turn it in to earn five free points. The five words were from an online blog about college success. The students had two days to complete an assignment that should have taken less than five minutes and bring it back to the next class.

Most students did the assignment and earned their five points. A few students went above and beyond the assignment by providing their own commentary on the blog. For those students, I gave an additional point or two.

But more than 28% of the students across all of my classes didn't bother to turn in the free assignment at all. I was shocked and disappointed at the level of apathy displayed by such a large percentage of my students. And some of those same students came to me later in the semester to plead their case for extra work so they could bring up their grades. I did not grant that request.

When I became a dad, I learned that the hard lessons are the ones which have molded my own children into the excellent college students and responsible adults that they have become. In a society where so many people feel that they are entitled to receive whatever they believe they deserve, I stand in direct opposition to that philosophy. I want my students to succeed. And the only way to succeed is to experience failure along the way. This is a painful lesson to learn, but it is one that everyone needs to understand if they are going to succeed in college, in a career, and in life. While I would prefer that my students take my word for it, many of them will have to experience it for themselves to understand that I am not overstating the problem.

I only hope that they learn this lesson now while they are young and can make adjustments. Because if not, they WILL learn it the hard way, when they are called into their boss's office and fired because they didn't complete a work assignment.

Don't pass up free points!

WATCH YOUR LANGUAGE

This next tip for college success is likely to ruffle some feathers. Some of you may even be inclined to ignore it—or cuss me out for it. But I urge you to consider the suggestion seriously.

Be careful with your use of profanity. Here's why:

Recently, one of my students (let's call her Samantha) came to my office to talk to me about career options. Much to her surprise, she was doing well in my math class and found herself enjoying the subject more than she ever had before. She started asking me questions about careers in mathematics, what future courses she might take, and what she could do with a degree in mathematics (a LOT!!!) even if she decided not to go into a purely mathematics-based field.

Samantha left my office greatly encouraged, and I was elated that one of my students was having such a positive experience in my class that she was actually considering mathematics as a profession. I was extremely impressed by Samantha's eloquence, intelligent questions, and deep thoughtfulness about where her future might lead. As she left my office, I thought to myself, "Samantha has a bright career in front of her."

A few days later, Samantha completely derailed my confidence in her future.

I walked into my classroom. As usual, students were milling around, finding their seats, and chatting. As I started to erase the chalkboard, I overheard Samantha talking to a couple of her friends. It was just general conversation—she was talking about what she did over the weekend. But as she spoke, I was shocked that nearly every other word was a profanity. F-bombs were dropping left and right, sprinkled in with less vulgar, but equally profane swear words. It was clear that this was simply a part of Samantha's normal pattern of conversation. She wasn't cussing anyone out. She was just talking. And I immediately felt sad. My expectations for her dropped a few notches in that moment.

Now before you chalk me up as just an old guy who doesn't relate to the current generation of young people, hear me out. Most of the people hiring the next generation of career-minded young men and women are old guys (or girls) just like me. They are looking for competence, excellence, dedication, and *professionalism* in their employees. And one of the quickest ways to turn off an employer is to use profanity, especially if it flows naturally from your lips as part of your normal conversation.

Most people will argue that they would never use that kind of language in a professional setting—ESPECIALLY in a job interview. I contend that when profanity is such a natural part of your conversation that you use it all the time, it will slip into your conversation occasionally, regardless of the situation. In fact, high stress situations like job interviews are exactly the conditions under which a slip would occur.

I remember a cocky young man who was doing a monologue for a Christmas Eve service at our church some years ago. He didn't practice his lines as well as he needed to, despite my encouragement that he be more diligent in his preparation. When he forgot one of his lines in the middle of his monologue, he began to ad-lib, and a mild profanity slipped into his monologue—in the middle of the service. Needless to say,

"PROFANITY ALIENATES PEOPLE, HURTS YOUR BRAND, AND SIMPLY DOESN'T WORK."

THAT was an uncomfortable moment. And the young man was extremely embarrassed. The problem is that the word he used was a normal part of his everyday language, so when he was under stress, it slipped out at the worst possible moment.

Best-selling author, blogger, and speaker Michael Hyatt said it best in a brilliant blog post. Hyatt states,

> *"Profanity alienates people, hurts your brand, and simply doesn't work[1]."*

How right he is. I realized this very recently when I decided to narrow down the number of "virtual mentors" that I follow online.

There are so many excellent people to learn from online who are speaking, leading, and making an impact. I simply do not have the capacity to follow all of them, so I decided to slowly eliminate some of them from my learning schedule. The first ones that I eliminated were those who freely sprinkle profanity in with their teaching. They may be killing it in the business field (in most cases, they are millionaire speakers and authors), but every time they speak, I cringe at their language. I cannot learn from them as easily when their profanity distracts me from their message.

I recognize that many professors use equally profane language in their classes. This is not about them. It's about you. As you reflect on your speaking style, I would encourage you to consider how your persona is reflected by the language you use. Do the words you use portray the professional image that you want to project? Do they reflect your intelligence level? Could they be hindering your potential growth and development?

WORK TO IMPROVE YOUR WRITING SKILLS

This is one of the most important tips in this entire chapter on college success. We live in a strange new society where we can carry on conversations with multiple different people at the click of a button or the swipe of a thumb.

Unfortunately, what has been lost in this brave new world of instant connectivity is the ability to write effectively. Spell-check and grammar check software built into our computers has effectively dumbed down our society's need to know how to write effectively.

In my opinion, the most important writing skill that has been lost is the ability to punctuate a sentence properly. Texting has become ubiquitous, and unfortunately, "text-speak" and its associated lack of proper grammar and punctuation has made its way into the writing skills of an entire generation of students.

I periodically teach an orientation course for new freshman. It's called "Foundations for Lifelong Learning," but it could just as easily be called "How to be a College Student 101." An important outcome of the course is for each student to write a short research paper. We build the paper piece-by-piece. We start with the cover page, then develop resources, create a bibliography, find three principle themes to build the paper around, write an introduction, and finally, create a conclusion that ties the themes together.

Unfortunately, the first thing I have to teach is how to use verbs properly, where to place proper punctuation, and how to clean up spelling errors. These are all concepts that have been taught from elementary school through high school, and yet, I have incoming college students who do not know how to write.

Even though many students don't like to write, it is a critical skill for your current and future success. Chances are high that you will be required to write research papers in multiple courses during your college career. And you better believe your psychology professor *will* take points off for bad grammar, spelling, and lack of punctuation!

Remember "there," "their," and "they're" are three different words—all with different meanings. The same goes for "your," "you're," and "yore." Make sure you know how to use these words (and other homonyms) correctly, or you will drive your professors crazy!

In your very first semester, you should take an elementary composition course. Nearly every college degree requires it, and it is one of the most easily transferable courses, should you choose to go to another college.

DEVELOP EFFECTIVE STUDY HABITS

Studying is critical to every student's success. While this might seem an obvious statement, many students do not take the proper steps to ensure that they are optimizing their study habits. One of the most important parts of effective studying is creating an effective study environment. Doing homework while lying across your bed or trying to write up a paper for your professor while sitting in your comfy chair is typically not the best way to increase your level of productivity. To work most effectively, you need to emulate the posture and position that you normally use when you are at work or school.

As an instructor, this meant getting out of my La-Z-Boy recliner and creating a comfortable, yet professional home office. My family gifted me with a beautiful roll-top desk for my birthday a couple of years ago, and the addition of an office chair, office supplies, and a bookshelf provided me with everything I needed to work efficiently from home.

As a student, you can cost-effectively create a similar space for doing homework by scanning Craigslist or local thrift stores for a good used desk and chair set. Rearranging your bedroom to make an "office" space will be worth the effort, and the reward for sacrificing a corner of your room to an "office" will show up in improved performance and better grades. Sitting at a desk helps the brain to take more seriously the task you are performing, thus increasing your productivity over the long haul.

My wife and I homeschool our children, so closing the door to my office is important for my productivity. When the door is open, I am distracted every time someone walks by. Also, the natural rhythm of the household tends toward noise and organized chaos. This isn't a bad thing. But it does tend to pull my focus from my work. Even as I write this, I hear my twelve-year old daughter singing while she clears the breakfast dishes from the dining room table. It's a lovely sound, and perfectly timed to make this point.

Just because the door is closed should not mean that you are inaccessible to the family. If anyone needs me for any reason, they need simply knock on the door and I'll be available for whatever is needed. But it does remind the kids that dad is working and he shouldn't be disturbed unless it's necessary.

Sometimes, if the kids are being particularly loud, I'll pop on a pair of headphones and listen to music or white noise (like the sound of a thunderstorm or waves crashing on the beach). I have found white noise to be particularly helpful when I am working.

FOLLOW YOUR REGULAR ROUTINE: This is the critical piece for my personal "work from home" productivity success. I need to maintain the same routine when I am working from home as I do when I go to the office.

Most people don't know this, but I'm a "sweatpants and t-shirt" kind of guy. When I get home from work, I immediately change out of my khakis and button-down shirts into sweats (or pajama pants) and a t-shirt. I'm just more relaxed that way, so it's easy for me to dress that way when I am working from home. But I have discovered that my brain slides into a less focused, more relaxed mindset when I do so. It's more difficult to concentrate when I am dressed more casually, and my output suffers because of it. At the end of those days, I look back on a day that wasn't as productive as it should have been—and I get frustrated.

When I plan a "work from home" day, I follow the same routine that I do on mornings when I go to the office. I get up at the same time that I normally do (for me, that is between 5:00 and 5:30). I shower and get dressed as if I am going to the office. The most important part of this routine for me is to put on my shoes. There is something about putting on shoes that says to me, "You are going to work. This isn't a casual day to lie around." Some people may find this a bit silly, but don't knock it until you try it!

When I walk into my home office dressed in my work clothes and close the door behind me, my brain clicks into "work mode" and I get more done than I do on the days where I stumble around the house in sweatpants. And when I lie down to sleep at night, I can look back with satisfaction on a day that was productive and fulfilling—the best kind of workday to have.

Maybe studying from home is not an option for you. Can you find a place that will provide an environment conducive to study? It would be helpful if you can find a consistent study location, as your brain will become trained to click into "study mode" whenever you go to that place.

How can you create an effective study environment that will minimize distractions and maximize your focus? Are there techniques that you can put into place to make your study times the most effective? Experiment with different options until you find the best study situation for you.

UTILIZE THE TUTORING CENTERS

Every college campus has resources available for student tutoring. The most common tutoring labs—even on small commuter campuses—are the math and writing centers.

These tutoring centers often seem to be free. In other words, no one is hitting you up for an hourly fee when you walk in for help. But make sure to check your bursar bill. Often, a tutoring center is paid for with fees buried in your student account. At my university, if you are enrolled in a 100-level math course, there is a $45 fee for math center support. So, in other words, you are paying a fee for the math center whether you use it or not.

While this might initially seem unfair, think of it this way: if you were to use the math lab just once a week for an *hour*, over a 15 week semester, you just received math tutoring assistance for only $3.00 per hour. That's a steal! Most tutors will charge a minimum of $15.00 per hour. And of course, the more you use the tutoring center, the better the deal. The tutors are usually students, just like you, who have already taken the courses for which you need their help. Don't dismiss the opportunity to use tutoring centers for additional assistance with homework and in preparation for exams.

YOU *CAN* GRADUATE EARLY!

According to an article in The New York Times, only 19% of students complete a four-year college degree in four years at most public universities. Fewer than 10% of the 580 public universities in the United States graduate more than half of their students in four years. And many college advisers are using six-year benchmarks for graduating with a bachelor's degree and three years for an associate degree[2].

Does that mean you are destined to take more than four years to complete a degree? Not necessarily. It means that if you are pursuing a bachelor's degree, you are *likely* to spend far more time (and money) earning that degree than you thought when you graduated from high school.

However, there is some good news. Here are five tips that can help cut down the time it will take for you to earn that degree. You may even earn it in fewer than four years, if you are disciplined:

TAKE DUAL-CREDIT COURSES: If you are still in high school, look for opportunities to maximize the value of your high school classes. Many colleges work in partnership with their state high schools to offer "dual-credit" classes, courses that will count for both high school and college credit. Find out what your school offers and earn that college credit while you are still in high school. Even if you don't plan to attend the college that offers the dual credit opportunities, you may be able to transfer the college credits to the university of your choice. Dual-credit opportunities exist for many high school courses, including math, history, English, and science classes, to name a few. It is not unusual for some students to begin their college careers with an entire semester's worth of credit hours under their belts!

AVOID REMEDIAL COURSES: According to the National Center for Public Policy and Education, "Every year in the United States, nearly 60% of first-year college students discover that, despite being fully eligible to attend college, they are not ready for post-secondary studies. After enrolling, these students learn that they must take remedial courses in English or mathematics, which do not earn college credits[3]."

Here are a couple of good suggestions for how you may be able to avoid remedial courses:

- **Take a math class during your senior year of high school:** Most high school math requirements can be completed by your junior year of high school and students are relieved that they do not have to take a math class when they are seniors. I elected not to take a math class as a senior, and it was not the smartest decision I have ever made! Students often forget material that they are not actively working on. By the time their college placement exam comes around, they have forgotten how to use the quadratic formula or the Pythagorean Theorem. They end up in a remedial algebra class in college, even though they got a "B" in Precalculus during their junior year of high school. And they end up paying more money and taking more time to get their degree, just because they wanted to avoid a year of math in high school.

- **Take your placement exams seriously:** This is the actual text of an e-mail I received from a student who tested into a remedial class and wanted to get into a course I was teaching that was required for her major:

  "Mr. Becker, I really did not know that the placement exam would have been such a big deal. I almost did not even take it. When taking the exam I can say that I really do not even remember taking my time or reading all the questions. I did not think that the placement exam would hurt me so much. If I can take it again I am ready to take it right now!"

What this student failed to understand is that a placement test is not something you are allowed to take and re-take (like a driver's test) until you pass it. Your success (or failure) on your placement exams will determine your starting point when you get to college. You could start out a semester behind, right on schedule, or even start out ahead of the game if your placement tests indicate that you might be able to test out of a class or two! Which brings us to the third tip:

TEST OUT OF COURSES: Students who are gifted in a particular academic area should use this to your advantage. If you have developed fluency in a foreign language, ask if you can test out of introductory language classes. Are you a history buff? Determine whether you can test out of any history courses. Most departments will offer opportunities to test out of classes if you demonstrate a competency in those areas.

BUT WHAT IF I'M ALREADY IN COLLEGE?: The previous tips primarily benefit students who have not yet begun their college career. But what if you are already into your first year of college and you are starting to realize that it may take you five or six years to graduate? Here are two tips to speed up the process:

- **Don't Stop at the Bare Minimum:** At most universities, 12 credits is the minimum number of credit hours you must take so that you qualify as a "full-time" student. Now do the math: if you take the minimum (12 credit hours) in the spring and the fall, you will only complete 24 credit hours in an academic year. You need 120 credit hours to get a degree. So, do some simple division: 120/24 = 5. It will automatically take you a minimum of five years to graduate if you only take the minimum number of credits each semester.

  Instead, consider adding just one class to your schedule each semester. This will take you from twelve to fifteen credit hours, or thirty credit hours per academic year. Now you can divide those 120 credits by thirty per year to graduate in four years!

- **Bulk Up for Summer:** Summer school gets a really bad rap when we are in high school. But for many college students, summer school is their best friend. The bad news is that classes are compact, usually only 6-8 weeks long. The GOOD news is that classes are compact, usually only 6-8 weeks long!!! You get them done quickly (like ripping off a Band-Aid), and taking just one or two classes during the summer can shave a semester (or more) off your college career—a huge financial savings for those who are watching their dollars.

I would caution you that taking summer school classes requires an even higher level of academic discipline than courses do during a regular semester. You will need to buckle down for those few weeks of summer school. That means even less time hanging out with friends or going to parties. If you have a part-time job, you might even need to request a temporary reduction in your work hours. But the payoff in terms of getting through college quicker will more than make up for a short term dip in your wages.

By implementing one or more of these tips, you can save yourself time as well as a TON of money. After all, the sooner you get your degree, the sooner you will start making money in that career starting job! College can still be a blast, but you can begin your career on the right foot with just a little strategic thinking and advanced preparation.

MANAGE YOUR MONEY EFFECTIVELY

One of the biggest mistakes I made as a young college student was to squander the money I had been given for school. I had plenty of money to get through several semesters, but I wasted it frivolously. Here are some suggestions for how to be responsible with your money when you become a college student.

SCHOLARSHIPS: Search high and low for scholarships when you are preparing to go to college. While the number of unclaimed scholarships is pretty low, they do exist. You may qualify for scholarships based on income, ethnicity, gender, academic ability, athletic ability, or any other number of factors.

If you research scholarships as if it were a part-time job, you could end up saving hundreds—or even thousands—of dollars.

PELL GRANTS: Unclaimed Pell Grants are actually far more common than unclaimed scholarships. A Pell Grant is money that is gifted to you by the government, based on a demonstrated financial need. It is not a loan, so you do not have to pay it back.

According to some sources, more than 2.6 billion dollars in Federal Pell Grants went unclaimed in 2018[4]. This is largely because thousands of high school students did not fill out their Free Application for Student Aid (FAFSA) forms in time for college enrollment.

FAFSA forms require information from the parents' income tax forms. Since the deadline for filing income tax returns is not until the middle of April, many students miss the deadline, and, in turn, miss out on over $5,900 in free money for college. The moral of this story—get your FAFSA done early!

WORK-STUDY: Many universities provide work-study positions to students who are enrolled full-time and have a demonstrated financial need. These are simply on-campus jobs that provide you an hourly salary—often with a semester or yearly cap. So, if the cap is $1,000 a semester and they pay $10.00/hour, a student could work 100 hours per semester to earn that money.

Work-study positions include secretarial work, IT support, receptionist duties, tutoring, or any variety of positions where the university may have a need. Check with the financial aid office for more information about work-study opportunities.

GET A JOB: The nice thing about work-study positions is that you have a job right on campus. Unfortunately, these opportunities are not always available. The next best thing is to get a part-time job close to your home or close to the campus.

I will caution you that going to college *full-time* is a *full-time* job (that's why they call it *full-time*). It is extremely difficult (and completely ill-advised) to try to hold a full-time job while also being a full-time student. Your schoolwork will suffer badly. And if you are enrolled as a full-time student, that means you are likely planning to find a new career after college. Don't jeopardize those career aspirations by doing something that will threaten your academic achievement.

I recommend that a full-time student tries to work only 12-15 hours a week. In extreme financial situations, I can see working as many as twenty hours per week, but don't try to do more than this. You are setting yourself up for failure and will more than likely burn yourself out.

STUDENT LOANS: Student loans are not necessarily a bad thing, but they should be used as a last option, after all other avenues have been explored. And you should only take the money that you *need*, not all of the money that you can get.

There are two types of student loans you can receive from the federal government: subsidized and unsubsidized loans. If you *must* take out loans, go for the subsidized ones over the unsubsidized. The reason is all about the interest that accrues on your loan.

In a subsidized loan, interest will not start to accrue on your loan until after you have graduated or been out of college for six months. This will save a lot of money over the repayment period. In an unsubsidized loan, interest begins to accrue from the moment the loan is taken out and continues throughout the repayment period.

My own story of student loan debt is a cautionary tale of why you need to be responsible when it comes to loans. Regrettably, I took out the maximum loans that I could (both subsidized and unsubsidized) and then used the excess cash (after tuition and books) for whatever I wanted. This came back to haunt me several years later. After graduation, I became a school teacher, and I wasn't making a lot of money. I had trouble making ends meet, and I defaulted on my student loans (that's a fancy way of saying that I stopped paying them). So, the United States government—who wasn't about to let me get away with their money—called the co-signers of my student loans—my parents. The loan officer told my mom and dad that since I wasn't paying off my student loans, they would have to do so.

I'm sure you can imagine the phone call I received from my parents about two minutes after they got off the phone with the government! Here I was, a "responsible" adult, married with two kids, and the debt collectors were calling mommy and daddy because Jonny wasn't paying his loans!

How embarrassing! As you can imagine, I apologized profusely to my parents, and I took a part-time job to catch up on my payments. I actually ended up paying off the loans early, and have made every effort to never be late on another payment of any kind.

TEXTBOOKS: Managing your money wisely can be difficult when you walk into the bookstore and find that your textbooks for the semester are going to cost more than $400.00. This is one of the sticker shock expenses of going to college. But there are a few things you can do to cut your textbook costs *dramatically*:

- **Buy Used:** If you want to own your textbooks, then look for used copies. They will be on the shelf right next to the shiny new textbooks, but they will be considerably cheaper.

- **Rent, Don't Buy:** If you don't care whether you own the book or not, then this is a terrific option. Most college bookstores will rent textbooks to you for as much as 50% of the purchase cost. However, you *must* return them in a timely fashion at the end of the semester, or the bookstore will charge your account for the balance of the cost that you would have paid to buy the book. This also means that you need to take care of the book. If you leave it out in the rain, heavily mark it up with highlighters, or tear out pages, you will not be allowed to return it and you will be charged for the balance.

- **Scour the Campus Bulletin Boards:** Students will often be unsatisfied with the buy-back price of the book at the campus bookstore. So, they will post books that they used for one semester on various (digital and actual) bulletin boards. You can often find fairly expensive books at deep discounts by tracking down students who had the same class last semester that you just enrolled in.

CONSIDER A NON-RESIDENTIAL CAMPUS: This next suggestion is often considered heresy by high school students who are itching to get out from under the rule of their parents. "I want my freedom!" is a common refrain from the soon-to-be high school graduate.

But freedom comes with a cost. And mom and dad might not be able to foot the bill for *your* desired freedom. Residential campuses carry a huge expense that non-residential colleges don't—it's called room and board, and it is often in excess of $10,000 per year for a state college.

But if you choose to live at home—even for just a couple of years—you can save a *lot* of money. And the courses you take during the first couple of years of college are largely general education courses that will apply to any degree you choose. In other words, you can get the same classes for your degree at a reduced cost.

An added benefit of choosing a non-residential campus is that the class sizes are often smaller, which means that you can develop more personal relationships with your professors.

While this might not seem important initially, good working relationships with professors could lead to possible job or research opportunities as well positive references for your resume. I actually got hired at Indiana University Northwest because the professors in the math department knew me from my time in the math education program.

CHAPTER TEN

"You will never change your life until you change something that you do daily. The secret of your success is found in your daily routine.

—*John C. Maxwell*

SO, YOU WANT TO SUCCEED AT LIFE?

In Chapter Nine, I outlined tips that will make your college experience much more successful. However, to cement your chances for success, you have to make changes in the way you live your life on a daily basis. You cannot continue to live an erratic lifestyle and expect radical change to occur.

This chapter looks at a variety of lifestyle "hacks" that will make it easier for you to experience the college (and life) success you're looking for.

RUTHLESSLY MANAGE YOUR TIME

What if your bank deposited $86,400 into your savings account every day? You would become rich very quickly...Unless...

What if there was a catch? What if, at the end of each day, they withdrew any balance that remained in the account? What would you do?

Well, if you're like me, you would probably go to the bank every day and withdraw all of the money so that the balance went back down to zero...

And the next day, they would make a new deposit...and you would go to the bank and withdraw all of the money...and so on...

Guess what? There IS a bank that does exactly that. Every day. It's called the Time Bank. And every day, whether we are the richest person in the world or the poorest, we each get the exact same deposit: 86,400 seconds. And we can spend those seconds any way that we want to.

But there's a catch. At the end of the day, we do not get to roll over to the next day any seconds that we have not used. They're gone.

If I were to waste money the way that I waste time, I would be broke very quickly. Often I do not even realize that I am wasting time. I do some part-time consulting to make a little extra income that helps meet our monthly budget...I get paid by the hour.

However, sometimes I find myself working—not because I need to—but because I am avoiding the things I need to do to accomplish my goals.

Often, I find myself sitting in front of the computer, consulting on some project or another, during the time I have set aside for other projects. And I rationalize it by thinking, "Well, we could use the money..." I can never get back the time that I spend on something else. And we are not given an unlimited number of daily deposits into our time bank.

How are you managing your time? Do you find yourself procrastinating? I recommend that you get yourself a planner—either digital or tactile (pencil and paper). I have used both systems and have found that I am most effective when I track my daily schedule in a written planner. There is something about the feel of the page and writing things out in longhand that helps me to be more productive and keep closer track of my time.

In Appendix B is a time log template. I encourage you to take one week and log your daily activities to see where you are spending your time. If you commit to diligently tracking your time usage for just one week, I am sure you will find the results to be eye-opening.

DEVELOP A DAILY START-UP RITUAL

One of the keys to success is consistency. To that end, I encourage you to develop a daily "start-up" ritual or routine. Michael Hyatt defines a ritual as "a prescribed procedure for achieving a specific result." This terrific definition gets right to the heart of your desire to turn your failure into success.

When I take control of my morning and stick to a "proactive start-up ritual," I get so much done, and I feel GREAT for the rest of the day. But when I fall into my "reactive start-up ritual," my focus wanders, and, just like a ship that drifts a few degrees off-course, I look back at my day and wonder how I ended up so far from my intended destination.

Let me describe what I mean:

My proactive morning ritual sounds like this:

1. Sit up as soon as the alarm goes off, stretch, say a brief prayer of thanks, and hit the shower.

2. Get dressed, make a protein shake or a cup of tea, and sit in my chair.

3. Write in my private journal.

4. Read my Bible and pray.

5. Open my computer and begin to write.

On the other hand, my reactive morning ritual sounds like this:

1. Hit the snooze alarm.

2. Hit the snooze alarm again.

3. Drag myself grumpily out of bed.

4. Stumble into the shower.

5. Stand under the hot water for at least ten minutes, hoping it will wake me up.

6. Get dressed, sit in my chair, and open my computer.

7. Surf the web for an hour.

I think you get the point.

Now in order for you to develop a proactive morning ritual, it's important that you examine how you currently start your day. With a pen and paper, take the next few mornings and document the time you get up in the morning, your habits as you begin your day, and the time when you first begin to work productively. Look for patterns that might be derailing your ability to get started and begin to eliminate them from your morning routine.

Once you have developed an effective morning ritual, you will be surprised how much more you will get done, as your productivity is likely to continue throughout the day.

LEARN TO SAY NO!

This is a companion skill to effective time management. As a people pleaser, I'm not good at saying no to people. Whenever I do, it's kind of a big deal for me.

Recently, I said no to a request for a letter of peer review. A peer review letter means I observe another faculty member's class, taking note of their teaching style, their interactions with students, and the educational environment they create (or don't create) within their classroom, and then I write a fairly detailed letter (presumably supporting their quest for promotion, tenure, or whatever goal they are seeking to achieve). It's a show of respect to be asked to write one of these, but I said no.

This wasn't as easy as it might sound. The request came from the dean of their school. This was not a small request. So saying no was not a small deal, but I did.

The reason is not that I think the other faculty member is a bad teacher. To be honest, I have never seen him teach. We have met a few times at university functions, and I know he is committed to excellence in teaching, based on his regular attendance at teaching conferences.

I said no because I examined my priorities...I reflected on the things I was already committed to. I looked at the *time* requirements necessary to complete this task within the time parameters necessary.

And I thought about the reasons why I would WANT to do the observation. There was only one reason I wanted to do it. I didn't want to let down the dean of the other school... the dean who I have never met.

I have written plenty of letters for plenty of people. I won't necessarily say no if this dean asks me again in the future for help with something like this. But I did on that day. I had to.

The other professor's teaching schedule was not at a time that was convenient for me...the service commitments I had already made were far too time-consuming to add another commitment. And that means I would have had to dig further into my personal time to do the job effectively.

I said no. I drew the line at my personal time. And I felt good about it. I cordially thanked the dean for the request. I respectfully declined, stating the reasons why I was unable to perform the task, and I recommended another person on campus that I respect and who I believed would do an excellent job. I handled this politely, professionally, and collegially.

I managed my personal time effectively. The dean was disappointed, but gracious. And I learned that saying no is not as difficult as I thought it would be.

As someone committed to your own success, you need to learn when to say no. It is not always easy. But it is critical to your future achievements.

You might need to say no to a group of friends who want to go to a movie when you need to study for an exam. You might need to say no to picking up extra hours at work when that shift conflicts with your class. Or you might need to say no to a job opportunity that seems good on its face but doesn't move you toward your desired goals.

Saying no is hard. But it will become easier as you practice it. And saying no is critical to your future success.

You need to make a decision: are you going to disappoint a few people in the short term by saying no to requests that do not fit your goal pursuits? Or are you going to disappoint yourself in the long term by saying yes to everyone's needs but your own?

Choose wisely. If you don't learn to say no to other people, you will always be saying no to yourself. And you will fail to realize the dreams and goals you have set for yourself.

BEGIN A READING PROGRAM

"Not all readers are leaders, but all leaders are readers."

—Harry S. Truman

According to an article by journalist Jeff Jarvis, the number of books being read by the average American is on the decline. He states the following statistics:

- One-third of high school graduates never read another book for the rest of their lives.

- 58% of the US adult population never read another book after high school.

- 42% of college graduates never read another book.

- 80% of US families did not buy or read a book last year.

- 70% of US adults have not been to a bookstore in the last five years.

- 57% of new books are not read to completion.

- Most readers do not get past page eighteen in a book they have purchased.

- Customers 55 and older account for more than one-third of all books bought.

Now, before you say, "Why should I read if I don't have to?" or "I don't like to read," consider the following benefits of reading from a podcast by Michael Hyatt.[1]

READING MAKES US BETTER THINKERS: When we read, we are actively studying how other people think. This informs our own thinking by helping us view life from another person's perspective. Hyatt suggests that when we read, we don't always need to focus on retention of content. Reading helps to broaden our thinking, strengthen our opinions, and make us more discerning.

READING IMPROVES OUR PEOPLE SKILLS: Have you ever been to a party where you encountered an extremely interesting person who seemed to be filled with fascinating information? Chances are excellent that this person is a reader. People who read regularly have more knowledge to draw from. Novels, history, and biographies are excellent information sources, and people who read are usually more interesting people with whom to have a conversation.

READING HELPS US MASTER COMMUNICATION SKILLS: According to Anne E. Cunningham, Professor of Education at Berkeley, books use 2-3 times the number of rare words as television. Simply stated, reading increases your vocabulary, making us more effective communicators.

READING HELPS US TO RELAX: Reading has been proven to lower our heart rates and relieve tension in as little as six minutes. It takes our mind off our own problems, slows our brains, and helps us to focus on something else. In fact, reading has a higher rate for proven stress relief than listening to music, drinking a cup of tea, or taking a walk. Dr. David Lewis, a cognitive neuropsychologist at the University of Sussex in England, said:

"Losing yourself in a book is the ultimate relaxation."

Some people use the excuse that they don't have time to read. But in this age of digital technology, we can download audio books to listen to while we are driving, cycling, or working out at the gym. The opportunity to absorb new content is no longer limited to the written page. And nearly any book you can imagine is probably available as a digital audio download. Libraries continue to increase the number of CD books for check-out, and online services like www.audible.com allow you to download books as mp3 files for a monthly fee.

Set a goal this week to find one book that interests you and dive in. It might be a novel, a self-help or business book, a biography, or a memoir of

"LOSING YOURSELF IN A BOOK IS THE ULTIMATE RELAXATION."

your favorite Hollywood celebrity. Schedule some time to put down your cell phone, close your Facebook feed, and allow yourself to be transported to another place or time through the wonder of reading.

MAKE A LIST

I am a list-making fiend. I make daily, weekly, monthly, quarterly, and yearly lists. That might sound a bit extreme to some people, but when I make my list of goals at the beginning of a year, the only way that I will come close to accomplishing those goals is to break them down into quarterly "chunks." I then break those quarterly "chunks" into monthly, then weekly, and, eventually daily chunks. It can get mighty difficult to track all of your lists if you don't have a system. This is where the use of a planner is vital.

I have tried a variety of planning systems to track my calendar, take notes, and keep a task list. Digital task managers like Wunderlist©, Todoist©, MS Outlook©, and Google Calendar© all offer excellent features that attract thousands, if not millions, of users. I have tried a variety of digital planners, and I have come to the realization that I just prefer to use an analog planner. There is something organic and natural to me about sitting down with a cup of coffee, a pen, and my planner to lay out my calendar for the upcoming year, quarter, month, or week.

Of course, just as there are a variety of digital planning resources to consider, there are an equal number of analog planners available. Day Timer©, The Bullet Planner©, and the Franklin Covey© planner are a few of the more popular ones. I used the Covey planner for a number of years, and I enjoyed it very much. However, a couple of years ago, Michael Hyatt released his Full Focus Planner© (FFP©), an aptly named analog tool that has revolutionized the way I track my busy schedule.

The FFP© is a quarterly planner that helps the user set and achieve goals, all within the context of their daily schedule. The front of the planner includes a section to write out multiple goals for the year (broken down into quarterly chunks), as well as a way to track your goals on a daily basis. Additionally, each week is preceded by a short section where you set your "Weekly Big 3" goals. Then, the daily pages provide a space for you to write your "Daily Big 3," the things you need to accomplish on a daily basis to help you accomplish your Weekly Big 3. Each day builds upon the previous one, and eventually, the diligent FFP© user finds himself or herself accomplishing goals that may have seemed too big to tackle initially.

One of the best features of the Full Focus Planner© is that there is a Facebook© group where FFP© users share tips, ask questions, and encourage one another on the road to success. There is also an entire series of videos—hosted by Michael Hyatt personally—that explain how to use each section of the planner to achieve maximum success. And Hyatt's support team is excellent. Invariably, they respond to e-mail questions within 24 hours—often less.

For some people, buying a planner might seem unnecessary. For those who are extremely practical, a simple legal pad and a pen may be all that is needed to get organized. There's nothing wrong with that. But it is vital to your success that you develop some sort of system for planning and tracking your life. And the more successful you become, the more that other people will put demands on your time. At that point, the need for some type of detailed planner will become a necessity.

USE SOCIAL MEDIA WISELY

Facebook©, Instagram©, Twitter©, and Snapchat© can all be very effective tools in your quest to achieve success. But they can become tools of self-destruction if they are not used wisely. I continue to be amazed by the number of people who ruin relationships—and even their careers—by posting stupid stuff online.

Recently, a number of high profile athletes, entertainers, and politicians have had to come forward and explain comments and pictures they posted on their social media accounts. Some of these posts occurred more than ten years ago. In one account, the athlete in question tried to "scrub" his account—deleting numerous comments that he had posted in *high school*—before deleting the account entirely. Unfortunately (for him), others had taken screenshots of his more offensive posts. When he became a high profile athlete, those posts were released for the world to see. While *his* account no longer contained the offensive materials, they still existed in cyberspace. And they were used to expose some unsavory things that he thought and said when he was only sixteen years old.

Here's a good rule to follow: every time you are going to post something on social media, tell yourself that your comments and pictures will be out there for the world to see FOREVER. Then ask if what you are posting is something that could come back to hurt you in the future.

You also need to be careful of what other people post about you. In today's society, nearly everyone carries a camera—something that was unheard of just twenty years ago. People can take a picture of you that you don't even know exists and post it on their own social media accounts. They can also tag the image with your name.

Now imagine that you have graduated from college and are looking to launch your career. Every human resource office where you apply for a job will Google© your name and do a social media check to see if anything that they deem offensive—or even simply unprofessional—pops up. And if it does, you may not receive an offer to interview. And the worst part is that you may never know the reason! Your resume might go straight into the garbage without a second thought. Potential employers are looking for people who will best represent their organization in a competent and professional manner. They are not going to hire someone who makes potentially offensive comments or shows up in compromising photos on social media.

If your social media accounts contain anything that *might* reflect negatively on you or your character, start to scrub your account immediately, and don't make any more questionable posts. It might be too late for some of the stuff that's already out there (depending on who your "friends" are), but you should still clean up your accounts ASAP.

PROMOTE YOURSELF

This is one of the hardest things I have ever had to do. My parents always taught me to be humble—that promoting myself makes me look arrogant and will turn off the very people that I am trying to impress.

In many ways, this is true. But after a number of years at the university, I learned that I could actually promote my skills and abilities—and, in turn, position myself for good things to happen—without coming off as proud, boastful, or arrogant.

For example, when I won our university's campus-wide award for teaching excellence, I didn't come in and apply for it during my first semester. I spent four years teaching classes, developing my skills as a teacher, and cultivating relationships with other professors and administrators who could help me to become a better instructor.

Eventually, my teaching skills improved. Students began to tell their friends that I was the one they should take for their math class. Soon, my classes were filling up before anyone else's. Administrators took notice, and I started to develop a reputation as an excellent teacher. It was *then* that I elected to pursue a teaching award—and only because I was urged to do so by a colleague.

I took three steps to win my first teaching award:

- **I did my job well:** When I went into the classroom, I sought to be the very best teacher I could be.

- **I developed relationships:** Initially, I developed positive relationships with my students. Eventually, those students started telling other students to enroll in my classes. Administrators noticed, and I began to develop relationships with *them*.

- **I built my reputation over time:** My reputation grew with no promotion on my part. I simply did my job, and over time, people began to notice me.

I was actually surprised when Robin, the chair of the teaching awards committee, came to me and told me that I had been nominated for the award. I thought I was being humble when I told her that there were too many other good teachers who deserved to win far more than me.

Robin pushed back on my false humility. She told me that when a student nominates a professor for an award like this, it is an incredible honor. The nominee should feel a responsibility to respect that student by pursuing the award.

Candidly, I was uncomfortable with applying for the nomination, because I knew that I would have to write a supporting file that would explain to the committee why I was deserving of the award. In other words, I had to promote myself.

It was very difficult to do. But what made it easier was the fact that I wasn't showing up out of nowhere and applying for a teaching excellence award. I had done the work over time (without even realizing it), and my reputation supported my application. I won the award, and I accepted it with genuine humility.

I have since won a few other awards, and I have been asked to serve on campus committees that highlight excellence in teaching. None of those opportunities would have come to me if I had not been willing to take a risk and promote myself.

LISTEN TWICE AS OFTEN AS YOU SPEAK

My mom always told me that God gave us two ears and one mouth because we should listen twice as often as we speak. While it's an old saying, there is a nugget of truth in it.

Nothing will help you build relationships better with your friends, colleagues, and bosses than your willingness to listen. It takes a certain level of self-awareness to apply this rule—especially when we find ourselves in a new situation. Nervousness will often take control of our mouths, and we will find ourselves talking nonstop, just to fill any dreaded silence that might arise.

If you find yourself in such a situation, take a deep breath to calm your nerves, and then ask a simple, open-ended question. Any question will do, as long as it cannot be answered with a simple yes or no. This will get the other person to start talking. And while they talk, make a genuine effort to listen. Maintain eye contact, nod occasionally, and make a point to remember some of the key themes of their story. You can use those themes to ask follow-up questions and develop a deeper conversation. They may employ the same technique with you. Eventually, your nervousness will fade and you will find yourself much more at ease.

This is a particularly effective technique to use in a job interview. While the person interviewing you may want to ask *you* most of the questions, you can show them that you are interested in other people by asking them questions as well.

ALL GOOD THINGS MUST COME TO AN END

It is my sincerest hope that this book has been a "good thing" for you to read.

I encourage you to put your life into proper perspective by reminding you of my own experiences. I'm no more or less special than the highest paid athlete in the world. I'm not better or worse than the most famous celebrities in Hollywood. And I am no better or worse than you. I'm just a regular guy who got kicked out of college and then decided that my biggest failure was not going to define the rest of my life.

Everything I have achieved has flowed from that one simple concept—failure will not define who I am or what I become.

As you pursue your own path in life, you *will* fail along the way—make no mistake about it. Whether you fail in school, your career, or a relationship, you will have a decision to make. Will you allow your failure to pull you into an abyss of depression, self-pity, and hopelessness? Or will you pick yourself up, shake off the disappointing emotions of your experience, and get back on the path to success?

As you process through your own circumstances, it is my sincerest hope that this book has given you some tools to help you on your own path.

Now go, take action, and turn your big failure into *bigger* success!

APPENDIX A

"You are the average of the five people you spend the most time with."

—*Jim Rohn*

RELATIONSHIP INVENTORY

In the table below, list the names of the five people that you spend the most time with. Be specific and honest.

Name	Relationship to You	What Do They Do?

Now, spend some time reflecting on these people. Grab a pen and a pad of paper and answer the following questions about each person:

1. What are their long-term goals?

2. Do they have any habits that hinder their success?

3. Are they a source of encouragement to you?

4. Do you admire their lifestyle?

5. Would you want to emulate their work ethic?

6. Are they someone that you would want to use as a job reference on your resume?

Now list the five people in your life who encourage you and are a positive influence to you. Answer the same six questions for each of these individuals.

Name	Relationship to You	What Do They Do?

Compare the list on the previous page to the list above. Is there any overlap? If so, congratulations! You have identified and are associating with people who can help you achieve your goals.

If there is little to no overlap, then you have just created a new list of people to whom you need to connect more regularly. At the same time, you may need to consider limiting your time with those people who are not helping you to grow and improve yourself.

APPENDIX B

TIME LOG TEMPLATE

Use the template to track your schedule for a week to see how you are using your time. Then answer the questions on the following page.

	Monday	Tuesday	Wednesday	Thursday
5-6 AM				
6-7 AM				
7-8 AM				
8-9 AM				
9-10 AM				
10-11 AM				
11-12 PM				
12-1 PM				
1-2 PM				
2-3 PM				
3-4 PM				
4-5 PM				
5-6 PM				
6-7 PM				
7-8 PM				
8-9 PM				
9-10 PM				
10-1 PM				
11-12 AM				

	Friday	Saturday	Sunday
5-6 AM			
6-7 AM			
7-8 AM			
8-9 AM			
9-10 AM			
10-11 AM			
11-12 PM			
12-1 PM			
1-2 PM			
2-3 PM			
3-4 PM			
4-5 PM			
5-6 PM			
6-7 PM			
7-8 PM			
8-9 PM			
9-10 PM			
10-1 PM			
11-12 AM			

"Time is what we want most, but what we use worst."

—*William Penn*

QUESTIONS

1. What do I like most about the way I spent my time this week?

2. What time of the day was I most productive?

3. What time of the day was I least productive?

4. What do I want to do more of with my time?

5. What do I want to do less of with my time?

6. How many hours per week do I spend in classes?

7. How many hours per week do I spend studying or working on projects and assignments?

8. Am I happy with my weekday wake-up time? If not, when should I get up in order to make my days more productive?

9. Do I schedule my time proactively, or do I let outside influences determine how I spend my time?

10. Am I giving myself enough time for sleep?

11. What changes can I make to my schedule in order to achieve my goals?

NOTES

CHAPTER ONE

1. Robert Downey Jr On Addiction. (2018, February 20). Retrieved from https://iamsoberapp.com/blog/robert-downey-jr-sober-story/
2. Ibid.
3. From Addict to Avenger. (2015, May 5). Retrieved from https://uproxx.com/movies/robert-downey-jr-addict-to-avenger/
4. Drug Rehab Success Story: Robert Downey Jr. (2011, October 25). Retrieved from https://www.seabrook.org/blog/drug-rehab-success-story-robert-downey-jr/
5. 'Forbes' Billionaire List. (2012, March 15). Retrieved from https://www.huffingtonpost.com/2016/12/13/forbes-billionaire-list-rowling_n_1347176.html
6. Rowling, J.K. (2008, June 5). "The Fringe Benefits of Failure, and the Importance of Imagination." *The Harvard Gazette.*

CHAPTER TWO

1. Bernie Marcus & Arthur Blank. (2008, October 10). Retrieved from https://www.entrepreneur.com/article/197614
2. Actor Robert Downey Jr. Teaches that It's Never too Late to Change Your Life. Retrieved from http://www.

meant2live.net/2016/05/actor-robert-downey-jr-teaches-that-its.html

CHAPTER SIX

1. Than, Cynthia. (2017, March 31). Retrieved from https://www.inc.com/cynthia-than/dominos-admitted-their-pizza-tastes-like-cardboard-and-won-back-our-trust.html
2. Schwantes, Marcel. (2016, August 25). Retrieved from https://www.inc.com/marcel-schwantes/4-am-morning-most-productive-time-of-day.html
3. Peri, Camille. (2014, February 13). Retrieved from https://www.webmd.com/sleep-disorders/features/10-results-sleep-loss#1
4. Gunnars, Kris. (2017, June 4). Retrieved from https://www.healthline.com/nutrition/10-super-healthy-high-fat-foods
5. Fottrell, Quentin. (2018, August 4). Retrieved from https://www.marketwatch.com/story/people-are-spending-most-of-their-waking-hours-staring-at-screens-2018-08-01
6. Pandika, Melissa. (2016, August 22). Retrieved from https://www.rallyhealth.com/health/screen-time-affects-health
7. More Screen Time for Teens Linked to ADHD Symptoms. (2018, July 17). Retrieved from https://www.npr.org/sections/health-shots/2018/07/17/629517464/more-screen-time-for-teens-may-fuel-adhd-symptoms

CHAPTER NINE

1. Hyatt, Michael. (2015, March 27). Retrieved from https://michaelhyatt.com/profanity/
2. Lewin, Tamar. (2104, December 1). Retrieved from https://www.nytimes.com/2014/12/02/education/

most-college-students-dont-earn-degree-in-4-years-study-finds.html

3. Beyond the Rhetoric: Improving College Readiness Through Coherent State Policy. Retrieved from http://www.highereducation.org/reports/college_readiness/gap.shtml

4. Helhoski, Anna. (2018, October 16). Retrieved from https://www.nerdwallet.com/blog/loans/student-loans/2018-fafsa-pell-grant/

CHAPTER TEN

1. Hyatt, Michael. (2105, May 4). Retrieved from https://michaelhyatt.com/science-readers-leaders/

ACKNOWLEDGEMENTS

My name may be the one on the cover, but a project like this isn't completed without the massive input and support from a whole team of people! Special thanks to:

- My publisher: Kary Oberbrunner and his team at Author Academy Elite: The idea of publishing this book was a pipedream until they showed me how to make it happen.

- My editing team: Christine Berman, Jason Becker, and LeAnn Becker: Thanks for hacking your way through my awkward writing to make this book something worth reading.

- My cover designer: Tracy Van Dolder: Her creativity and unique style brought the cover to life in a way that I could never have envisioned.

- My mastermind group: Larry, Mark, Tom, Russell, and Bryan: Our meetings are the highlight of my week! Without your wisdom, encouragement, insight, and occasional bad humor (Mark), I could not have persisted through to see the end of this book.

- My spiritual advisor, mentor, and friend: Steve Buchelt: I'm not sure what you saw in me as a screwed-up high school kid, Steve. But I am so grateful that you chose to invest in me. I would not be the man I am today without your wisdom and guidance!

- My business mentor: Cliff Ravenscraft: The best life coach and most amazing motivator I could ever hope to have. Cliff, you rock!

- The professors who didn't give up on me: Lary Schiefelbusch, John Synowiec, Henry Wyzinski, Jim Boland, and Clyde Wiles mentored me through my return to college and showed me how to be a compassionate, caring, and fair teacher.

- My students: I have had the privilege of teaching literally thousands of students over the past thirty years. I'm grateful that, even as a veteran instructor, I continue to learn from them daily how to become an even better teacher.

- My lifelong friend Eric Berman: I have shared my heartiest laughs and my most inconsolable tears with you, Eric. My life is far richer for having you as one of my very best friends. Here's to forty more years of friendship!

- My kids: Jack and Kelsie, Kelly and Eric, Andrew, Matthew, Jason and LeAnn, Sarah, Faith, and Rachael—I'm a proud dad! I could never have completed this book without the cheerleading support of all of you.

- My wife: Katie-baby, you took a stand against mediocrity when we were just nineteen years old. The path my life has taken was first formed when you challenged me to be better than I was. You are the light of my life, and I absolutely adore you. Thank you for sticking with me through more than thirty years of marriage. I love you!

- And most importantly, thank you to my Lord and Savior, Jesus Christ, for the gift of salvation and forgiveness, without which I would be lost forever. 1 John 1:9.

To schedule Jon Becker for your next event

Visit

---

theflunkedoutprofessor.com

or call 219.765.7826

CPSIA information can be obtained
at www.ICGtesting.com
Printed in the USA
LVHW090128070219
606676LV00001B/4/P